THE
SECRET
WAY TO
WAR

THE DOWNING STREET MEMO AND THE IRAQ WAR'S BURIED HISTORY

MARK DANNER

THE
SECRET
WAY TO
WAR

THE DOWNING STREET MEMO AND THE IRAQ WAR'S BURIED HISTORY

PREFACE BY FRANK RICH

NEW YORK REVIEW BOOKS, NEW YORK

•

THIS IS A NEW YORK REVIEW BOOK

PUBLISHED BY THE NEW YORK REVIEW OF BOOKS

THE SECRET WAY TO WAR: THE DOWNING STREET MEMO
AND THE IRAQ WAR'S BURIED HISTORY
by Mark Danner

This edition published in 2006 in the United States of America by
The New York Review of Books, 1755 Broadway, New York, NY 10019
www.nybooks.com

Book and cover design by Milton Glaser, Inc.

Library of Congress Cataloging-in-Publication Data

Danner, Mark, 1958–.
   The secret way to war: the Downing Street Memo and Iraq's buried history /
by Mark Danner; preface by Frank Rich.
       p. cm. — (New York Review Books collections)
   ISBN 1-59017-207-8 (alk. paper)
       1. Iraq War, 2003—Causes. 2. Weapons of mass destruction — Iraq.
3. United States — Politics and government—2001 4. Great Britain—Politics
and government—1997 I. Rich, Frank. II. Title. III. New York Review Books
collection.
   DS79.76.D358 2006
   956.7044'31—dc22

                                                            2006000697

ISBN-10: 1-59017-207-8
ISBN-13: 978-1-59017-207-0

Printed in the United States of America on acid-free paper.

1 3 5 7 9 10 8 6 4 2

For my father,
who taught me to question

CONTENTS

PREFACE

IT'S HARD NOT TO THINK of Kazuo Ishiguro's novel *The Remains of the Day* when reading Mark Danner on what will forever be known as the Downing Street memo. Ishiguro told the story of a butler, just beyond the periphery of tawdry events in high places in World War II England, who pieces together fragment by fragment the story of his lord's collaboration with the Germans. So Danner, standing at a remove from momentous sotto voce conversations among the British ruling class on the eve of another war, teases out the meaning of similar evidence at his disposal until finally we get a clear and damning larger picture of a plot to take both England and the United States into a war of choice in Iraq on false premises. But you can only take this analogy so far. Unlike Ishiguro's tragically limited narrator, Danner understands the implications of every piece of the story, and, in these pages, lays out the history of "the secret way to war" with devastating acuity.

The Downing Street memo, first published by the *Sunday Times* of London on May 1, 2005, contains the secret minutes of a meeting Prime Minister Tony Blair held with his government's national security and foreign policy hierarchy in July 2002. "C," the head of British intelligence, reports on his findings from a recent visit with the equivalent players in Washington. Despite public claims that it would go to war in Iraq only as "a last resort," the Bush administration had months earlier decided to wage that war no matter what, "C" says. All that was missing was a way to sell it, and to do so, Washington was now engaged in a campaign to see to it that "the intelligence and facts" would be "fixed around the policy." That intelligence and those facts, of course, all pertained to Saddam Hussein's weapons of mass destruction, the war's ostensible casus belli, which we now know did not exist.

Out of this memo—indeed out of that one phrase in the memo—nearly everything else in the sordid story of the way to war flows: the refusal to allow the United Nations weapons inspectors to finish their work in Iraq, as Hans Blix and every American ally except England wanted; the activities of the so-called White House Iraq Group to publicize cherry-picked (and erroneous) intelligence produced outside the normal channels by what Lawrence Wilkerson, Colin Powell's former chief of staff, has called the Dick Cheney–Donald Rumsfeld cabal; the egregious "intelligence and facts" about weapons of mass destruction presented to the UN Security Council and the world by Powell; the parade of what Danner calls "increasingly lurid disclosures" by the Bush administration to the press about Saddam's doomsday weapons in the run-up to war; and the Valerie Plame Wilson leak case, which has revealed just how eager the White House was to punish anyone who might expose the extent to which the intelligence and facts had indeed been fixed on WMDs.

In retrospect, much of this subterfuge was hiding in plain sight. Yet the American press, much of which had been overly credulous in reporting the "evidence" of Saddam's weapons program to start with, was not particularly eager to correct the record when the fictions were exposed after the invasion. Like the public, which soured on the war in the invasion's aftermath, much of the American news media was eager to turn the page. When the Downing Street memo first surfaced in the British press, no major mass American journalistic outlet rushed to print the text in full or even to much deliberate about its contents. That job fell instead to *The New York Review of Books*. The detached and defensive view of even the sharpest of the so-called liberal American press can be seen most clearly in the extended exchange, included here, between Danner and Michael Kinsley, then the editorial page editor of the *Los Angeles Times*.

As Danner predicts, the number of Americans who believe that the President and his administration intentionally "misled the American public before the war" has steadily grown with each passing week since the revelation of the Downing Street memo. The press has since caught up with the public and is belatedly filling in every chapter in this duplicitous narrative that it can. But, as was also the case in his early commentaries for The New York Review on the documents delineating America's road to the practice of torture in Abu Ghraib and beyond, Danner was among the first to separate the threads of reality from the Alice-in-Wonderland fantasies the American government and its well-oiled propaganda machinery would have us believe. No other writer has done it with remotely his precision and deadpan wit.

—**FRANK RICH**

INTRODUCTION

RES IPSO LOQUITUR, I thought, when first I cast my eye on the so-called Downing Street memo: Let the thing speak for itself. What strikes one about the document—a two-and-a-half-page account of a meeting at 10 Downing Street in July 2002 in which Prime Minister Tony Blair and his "war cabinet" discuss the coming attack on Iraq—is its almost shocking clarity, the crystalline picture it provides of attitudes among senior British and American officials nearly eight months before bombs fall on Baghdad and tanks roll into Iraq. We see the British intelligence chief, just off the plane, report how in Washington war is "now seen as inevitable"; how it will be "justified by the conjunction of terrorism and WMD"; and how "the intelligence and facts were being fixed around the policy." We watch the British foreign secretary point out that "the case [for war] was thin"— "Saddam was not threatening his neighbours, and his WMD capability was less than that of Libya, North Korea or Iran"— and then listen as he suggests a way around this inconvenient fact: "We should work up a plan for an ultimatum to Saddam to allow back in the UN weapons inspectors...[to] help with the legal justification for the use of force." And we watch the prime minister immediately grasp the point of such a plan, and hear him agree that "it would make a big difference politically and legally if Saddam refused to allow in the UN inspectors."

And so on: in scarcely two and a half pages of impeccable English public school prose the Cabinet meeting is described and with it much of the story of how the United States and the United Kingdom went to war in Iraq. Priceless, I thought, reading the document for the first time on May 1, 2005; blessings upon whoever leaked these few thousand words to the London *Sunday Times*. No doubt the leaker was seeking to undermine the prime minister in the election campaign. No matter; the account was absolutely authoritative. Whatever the motives that prompted its release, *res ipso loquitur*.

Alas, we are living in an age, post–September 11, one of whose defining characteristics is precisely that things *don't* speak for themselves. Days passed and the Downing Street memo, which had caused an enormous stir in Great Britain, went virtually unnoticed in the United States. Coverage in the American press was sparse and, when it appeared at all, distinctly defensive. No newspaper saw fit to publish the document. After a few days I telephoned Robert B. Silvers, co-editor of *The New York Review of Books*, and suggested he put the memorandum in print. He agreed and asked for an essay to accompany it. That essay provoked letters (from a leading Washington reporter, from a well-known political pundit), which provoked in turn my responses, and soon the *Review* had published not one essay but three; and now this little book, which collects those three essays and follows them with the texts of eight British government documents, including that of the Downing Street memo itself.

Consisting as it does of a series of essays describing not only the memo but the reaction to it, the book is a treatment of scandal and of its disclosure. More precisely, the book shows in its unfolding, in its own movement of assertion and reaction, one of the signal characteristics of our particular age: that scandal survives its disclosure. In the shadow of the September 11 attacks and the permanent, twilight war that succeeded them, we find ourselves living in an Age of Frozen Scandal. The particular rhythm of public disclosure and investigation familiar from Watergate and after, the cycle of revelation, investigation, and expiation by which newspaper exposés lead to congressional investigation and thereby to trial, conviction, and punishment by the courts—this cycle, under pressure of war and a one-party government, has been short-circuited. We have become accustomed to a truncated cycle in which revelation of wrongdoing is followed by…nothing; or rather, nothing beyond the public knowledge of that wrongdoing. Official investigation, when it comes, tends to be severely circumscribed, either implicitly—as with the various military-led inquiries into the torture revelations, which have largely excluded the question of civilian policymakers' responsibility—or explicitly —as with the Senate Intelligence Committee's abbreviated inquiry into intelligence and the Iraq war, in which the central question of policymakers' use of that intelligence was placed outside the compass of inquiry and postponed to an indefinite future.

We are thus forced to live with the knowledge brought by the revelation; the political expiation of that wrongdoing, it appears, must await another time. The subject of this book, then, is not only the Downing Street memo and what it reveals but rather how Americans—the public and, most of all, the press—came to live with its revelation. In that sense it is a book not about what happened but about what is happening. In taking up this subject I have been greatly helped by the venerable tradition of the *New York Review of Books* "exchange" in which the *Review*'s editors encourage writers to engage with the arguments of those who read and comment on their work. Thanks to that tradition *The Secret Way to War*, which is based on a series of essays, and the response to those essays, published over three months, can not only describe but in a sense demonstrate an unfolding process whereby information critical to the public life of the country is both revealed and at the same time denied—brought to light and at the same time pushed back into the dark. Partly for this reason I have decided to leave the texts of these essays pretty much unaltered—to include them here much as they first appeared in print.

As I write, nearly three years after the Iraq war began, Americans have still had no authoritative, official account of how their country could have launched a war to destroy weapons that turned out not to exist. Perhaps the efforts of Senator Harry Reid, Democrat of Nevada and Senate minority leader, who shut down the Senate on November 1, 2006, to protest this state of affairs—specifically, the failure of the Senate Intelligence Committee to deliver the long-promised "Phase II" of its investigation of the use of intelligence on Iraq—will eventually lead to an authoritative investigation. More likely, as I discuss in a brief afterword, such an investigation will have to await a much broader and deeper change in the country's political dynamics. We shall see.

It remains for me to thank Michael Shae, who edited this book; Rea Hederman, who published it; and the editors and staff of The New York Review of Books, who encouraged me to write these essays and saw them through to print. I thank also my assistant nonpareil, Joshua Jelly-Schapiro, for essential help he provided in researching this work and for many astute comments he offered on earlier versions of the text. I am especially grateful to my longtime editor, Robert B. Silvers, who brought to bear his unparalleled enthusiasm, determination, and knowledge. This work would not exist without him.

Among the many things my father, Dr. Robert Danner, taught me was how to read the newspaper—which is to say: skeptically, always skeptically. By his words and his example he always insisted that the essence of being a real citizen lay in an unflagging determination to ask questions, and to demand answers. In love and gratitude I dedicate this little book to him.

—MDD

January 2006

THE

SECRET

WAY TO

WAR

As published in *The New York Review of Books*
June 9, 2005

THE SECRET WAY TO WAR

IT WAS OCTOBER 16, 2002, and the United States Congress had just voted to authorize the President to go to war against Iraq. When George W. Bush came before members of his Cabinet and Congress gathered in the East Room of the White House and addressed the American people, he was in a somber mood befitting a leader speaking frankly to free citizens about the gravest decision their country could make.

The 107th Congress, the President said, had just become "one of the few called by history to authorize military action to defend our country and the cause of peace." But, he hastened to add, no one should assume that war was inevitable. Though "Congress has now authorized the use of force," the President said emphatically, "I have not ordered the use of force. I hope the use of force will not become necessary." The President went on:

> Our goal is to fully and finally remove a real threat to world peace and to America. Hopefully this can be done peacefully. Hopefully we can do this without any military action. Yet, if Iraq is to avoid military action

by the international community, it has the obligation to
prove compliance with all the world's demands. It's the
obligation of Iraq.

Iraq, the President said, still had the power to prevent war by "declaring and destroying all its weapons of mass destruction"—but
if Iraq did not declare and destroy those weapons, the President
warned, the United States would "go into battle, as a last resort."

It is safe to say that, at the time, it surprised almost no one
when the Iraqis answered the President's demand by repeating
their claim that in fact there were no weapons of mass destruction. As we now know, the Iraqis had in fact destroyed these
weapons, probably years before George W. Bush's ultimatum:
"the Iraqis"—in the words of chief US weapons inspector David
Kaye—"were telling the truth."

As Americans watch their young men and women fighting
in the third year of a bloody counterinsurgency war in Iraq—
a war that has now killed more than 1,600 Americans[1] and tens
of thousands of Iraqis—they are left to ponder "the unanswered
question" of what would have happened if the United Nations

---

1. In January 2006, the number of Americans who had died in Iraq passed 2,200.
[*footnote added*]

weapons inspectors had been allowed—as all the major powers except the United Kingdom had urged they should be—to complete their work. What would have happened if the UN weapons inspectors had been allowed to prove, before the US went "into battle," what David Kaye and his colleagues finally proved afterward?

Thanks to a formerly secret memorandum published by the London *Sunday Times* on May 1, during the run-up to the British elections, we now have a partial answer to that question.[2] The memo, which records the minutes of a meeting of Prime Minister Tony Blair's senior foreign policy and security officials, shows that even as President Bush told Americans in October 2002 that he "hope[d] the use of force will not become necessary"—that such a decision depended on whether or not the Iraqis complied with his demands to rid themselves of their weapons of mass destruction—the President had in fact already definitively decided, at least three months before, to choose this "last resort" of going "into battle" with Iraq. Whatever the Iraqis chose to do or not do, the President's decision to go to war had long since been made.

On July 23, 2002, eight months before American and British

---

2. The reader will find the full text of the Downing Street memo beginning on page 87, along with seven related memoranda produced by the British government. [*footnote added*]

forces invaded, senior British officials met with Prime Minister Tony Blair to discuss Iraq. The gathering, similar to an American "principals meeting," brought together Geoffrey Hoon, the defence secretary; Jack Straw, the foreign secretary; Lord Goldsmith, the attorney general; John Scarlett, the head of the Joint Intelligence Committee, which advises the prime minister; Sir Richard Dearlove, also known as "C," the head of MI6 (the equivalent of the CIA); David Manning, the equivalent of the national security adviser; Admiral Sir Michael Boyce, the chief of the Defence Staff (or CDS, equivalent to the chairman of the Joint Chiefs); Jonathan Powell, Blair's chief of staff; Alastair Campbell, director of strategy (Blair's communications and political adviser); and Sally Morgan, director of government relations.

After John Scarlett began the meeting with a summary of intelligence on Iraq—notably, that "the regime was tough and based on extreme fear" and that thus the "only way to overthrow it was likely to be by massive military action," "C" offered a report on his visit to Washington, where he had conducted talks with George Tenet, his counterpart at the CIA, and other high officials. This passage is worth quoting in full:

> C̲ reported on his recent talks in Washington. There
> was a perceptible shift in attitude. Military action was

now seen as inevitable. Bush wanted to remove Saddam, through military action, justified by the conjunction of terrorism and WMD. But the intelligence and facts were being fixed around the policy. The NSC had no patience with the UN route, and no enthusiasm for publishing material on the Iraqi regime's record. There was little discussion in Washington of the aftermath after military action.

Seen from today's perspective this short paragraph is a strikingly clear template for the future, establishing these points:

1. By mid-July 2002, eight months before the war began, President Bush had decided to invade and occupy Iraq.
2. Bush had decided to "justify" the war "by the conjunction of terrorism and WMD."
3. Already "the intelligence and facts were being fixed around the policy."
4. Many at the top of the administration did not want to seek approval from the United Nations.
5. Few in Washington seemed much interested in the aftermath of the war.

We have long known, thanks to Bob Woodward and others, that military planning for the Iraq war began as early as November 21, 2001, after the President ordered Secretary of Defense Donald Rumsfeld to look at "what it would take to protect America by removing Saddam Hussein if we have to," and that Secretary Rumsfeld and General Tommy Franks, who headed Central Command, were briefing American senior officials on the progress of military planning during the late spring and summer of 2002; indeed, a few days after the meeting in London leaks about specific plans for a possible Iraq war appeared on the front pages of *The New York Times* and *The Washington Post*.

What the Downing Street memo confirms for the first time is that President Bush had decided, no later than July 2002, to "remove Saddam, through military action," that war with Iraq was "inevitable"—and that what remained was simply to establish and develop the modalities of justification; that is, to come up with a means of "justifying" the war and "fixing" the "intelligence and facts...around the policy." The great value of the discussion recounted in the memo, then, is to show, for the governments of both countries, a clear hierarchy of decision-making. By July 2002 at the latest, war had been decided on; the question at issue now was how to justify it—how to "fix," as it were, what Blair will later call "the political context." Specifically, though by this point in July the President had decided to go to war, he had not yet decided to go to the United Nations and demand inspectors; indeed, as "C" points out, those on the National Security Council—the senior security officials of the US government—"had no patience with the UN route, and no enthusiasm for publishing material on the Iraqi regime's record." This would later change, largely as a result of the political concerns of these very people gathered together at 10 Downing Street.

After Admiral Boyce offered a brief discussion of the war plans then on the table and the defence secretary said a word or two about timing—"the most likely timing in US minds for military action to begin was January, with the timeline beginning 30 days before the US Congressional elections"—Foreign Secretary Jack Straw got to the heart of the matter: not whether or not to invade Iraq but how to justify such an invasion:

> The <u>Foreign Secretary</u> said he would discuss [the timing of the war] with Colin Powell this week. It seemed clear that Bush had made up his mind to take military action, even if the timing was not yet decided. But the case was thin. Saddam was not threatening his

neighbors, and his WMD capability was less than that of Libya, North Korea or Iran.

Given that Saddam was not threatening to attack his neighbors and that his weapons of mass destruction program was less extensive than those of a number of other countries, how does one justify attacking? Foreign Secretary Straw had an idea:

> We should work up a plan for an ultimatum to Saddam to allow back in the UN weapons inspectors. This would also help with the legal justification for the use of force.

The British realized they needed "help with the legal justification for the use of force" because, as the attorney general pointed out, rather dryly, "the desire for regime change was not a legal base for military action." Which is to say, the simple desire to overthrow the leadership of a given sovereign country does not make it legal to invade that country; on the contrary. And, said the attorney general, of the "three possible legal bases: self-defence, humanitarian intervention, or [United Nations Security Council] authorization," the first two "could not be the base in this case." In other words, Iraq was not attacking the United States or the United Kingdom, so the leaders could not claim to be acting in self-defense; nor was Iraq's leadership in the process of committing genocide, so the United States and the United Kingdom could not claim to be invading for humanitarian reasons.[3] This left Security Council authorization as the only conceivable legal justification for war. But how to get it?

At this point in the meeting Prime Minister Tony Blair weighed in. He had heard his foreign minister's suggestion about drafting an ultimatum demanding that Saddam let back in the United Nations inspectors. Such an ultimatum could be politically critical, said Blair—but only if the Iraqi leader turned it down:

> The Prime Minister said that it would make a big difference politically and legally if Saddam refused

3. Humanitarian concerns might have been given as a reason for intervention in 1988, for example, when the Iraqi regime was carrying out its Anfal campaign against the Kurds; at that time, though, the Reagan administration—comprising many of the same officials who would later lead the invasion of Iraq—was supporting Saddam in his war against Iran and kept largely silent. The second major killing campaign of the Saddam regime came in 1991, when Iraqi troops attacked Shiites in the south who had rebelled against the regime in the wake of Saddam's defeat in the Gulf War; the first Bush administration, despite President George H. W. Bush's urging Iraqis to "rise up against the dictator, Saddam Hussein," and despite the presence of hundreds of thousands of American troops within miles of the killing, stood by and did nothing. See Ken Roth, "War in Iraq: Not a Humanitarian Intervention" (Human Rights Watch, January 2004).

to allow in the UN inspectors. Regime change and WMD were linked in the sense that it was the regime that was producing the WMD.... If the political context were right, people would support regime change. The two key issues were whether the military plan worked and whether we had the political strategy to give the military plan the space to work.

Here the inspectors were introduced, but as a means to create the missing casus belli. If the UN could be made to agree on an ultimatum that Saddam accept inspectors, and if Saddam then refused to accept them, the Americans and the British would be well on their way to having a legal justification to go to war, by means of the attorney general's third alternative: UN Security Council authorization.

Thus, the idea of UN inspectors was introduced not as a means to avoid war, as President Bush repeatedly assured Americans, but as a means to make war possible. War had been decided on; the problem under discussion here was how to make, in the prime minister's words, "the political context... right." The "political strategy"—at the center of which was weapons of mass destruction, for "it was the regime that was producing the WMD"—must be strong enough to give "the military plan the space to work." Which is to say, once the allies were victorious the war would justify itself. The demand that Iraq accept UN inspectors, especially if refused, could form the political bridge by which the allies could reach their goal: "regime change" through "military action."

But there was a problem: as the foreign secretary pointed out, "on the political strategy, there could be US/UK differences." While the British considered legal justification for going to war critical—they, unlike the Americans, were members of the International Criminal Court—the Americans did not. Mr. Straw suggested that given "US resistance, we should explore discreetly the ultimatum." The defence secretary, Geoffrey Hoon, was more blunt, arguing

> that if the Prime Minister wanted UK military involvement, he would need to decide this early. He cautioned that many in the US did not think it worth going down the ultimatum route. It would be important for the Prime Minister to set out the political context to Bush.

The key negotiation in view at this point, in other words, was not with Saddam over letting in the United Nations inspectors

—both parties hoped he would refuse to admit them, and thus provide the justification for invading. The key negotiation would be between the Americans, who had shown "resistance" to the idea of involving the United Nations at all, and the British, who were more concerned than their American cousins about having some kind of legal fig leaf for attacking Iraq. Three weeks later, Foreign Secretary Straw arrived in the Hamptons to "discreetly explore the ultimatum" with Secretary of State Powell, perhaps the only senior American official who shared some of the British concerns; as Straw told the secretary, in Bob Woodward's account, "If you are really thinking about war and you want us Brits to be a player, we cannot be unless you go to the United Nations."[4]

---

4. See Bob Woodward, *Plan of Attack* (Simon and Schuster, 2004), p. 162.

BRITAIN'S STRONG SUPPORT for the "UN route" that most American officials so distrusted was critical in helping Powell in the bureaucratic battle over going to the United Nations. As late as August 26, Vice President Dick Cheney had appeared before a convention of the Veterans of Foreign Wars and publicly denounced "the UN route." Asserting that "simply stated, there is no doubt that Saddam Hussein now has weapons of mass destruction [and] there is no doubt that he is amassing them to use against our friends, against our allies, and against us," Cheney advanced the view that going to the United Nations would itself be dangerous:

> A return of inspectors would provide no assurance whatsoever of his compliance with UN resolutions. On the contrary, there is great danger that it would provide false comfort that Saddam was somehow "back in the box."

Cheney, like other administration "hard-liners," feared "the UN route" not because it might fail but because it might succeed and thereby prevent a war that they were convinced had to be fought.

As Woodward recounts, it would finally take a personal visit by Blair to the White House on September 7 to persuade President Bush to go to the United Nations:

> For Blair the immediate question was, Would the United Nations be used? He was keenly aware that in Britain the question was, Does Blair believe in the UN? It was critical domestically for the prime minister to show his own Labour Party, a pacifist party at heart, opposed to war in principle, that he had gone the UN route. Public opinion in the UK favored trying to make international institutions work before resorting to force. Going through the UN would be a large and much-needed plus.[5]

The President now told Blair that he had decided "to go to the UN" and the prime minister, according to Woodward, "was relieved." After the session with Blair, Bush later recounts to Woodward, he walked into a conference room and told the British officials gathered there that "your man has got cojones." ("And of course these Brits don't know what cojones are," Bush tells Woodward.) Henceforth this particular conference

---

5. See Woodward, *Plan of Attack*, pp. 177–178.

with Blair would be known, Bush declares, as "the cojones meeting."

That September the attempt to sell the war began in earnest, for, as White House Chief of Staff Andrew Card had told The New York Times in an unusually candid moment, "From a marketing point of view, you don't introduce new products in August." At the heart of the sales campaign was the United Nations. Thanks in substantial part to Blair's prodding, George W. Bush would come before the UN General Assembly on September 12 and, after denouncing the Iraqi regime, announce that "we will work with the UN Security Council for the necessary resolutions." The main phase of public diplomacy—giving the war a "political context," in Blair's phrase—had begun. Though "the UN route" would be styled as an attempt to avoid war, its essence, as the Downing Street memo makes clear, was a strategy to make the war possible, partly by making it politically palatable.

As it turned out, however—and as Cheney and others had feared —the "UN route" to war was by no means smooth, or direct. Though Powell managed the considerable feat of securing unanimous approval for Security Council Resolution 1441, winning even Syria's support for bringing United Nations weapons inspectors back to Iraq, the allies differed on the key question of whether or not the resolution itself constituted UN approval for the use of force against Saddam, as the Americans contended, or whether a second resolution would be required, as the majority of the council, and even the British, conceded it would. Sir Jeremy Greenstock, the British ambassador to the UN, put this position bluntly on November 8, the day Resolution 1441 was passed:

> We heard loud and clear during the negotiations about "automaticity" and "hidden triggers"—the concerns that on a decision so crucial we should not rush into military action.... Let me be equally clear.... There is no "automaticity" in this Resolution. If there is a further Iraqi breach of its disarmament obligations, the matter will return to the Council for discussion as required.... We would expect the Security Council then to meet its responsibilities.

Vice President Cheney could have expected no worse. Having decided to travel down "the UN route," the Americans and British would now need a second resolution to gain the necessary approval to attack Iraq. Worse, Saddam frustrated British and American hopes, as articulated by Blair in the

July 23 meeting, that he would simply refuse to admit the inspectors and thereby offer the allies an immediate casus belli. Instead, hundreds of inspectors entered Iraq, began to search, and found...nothing. January, which Defence Secretary Hoon had suggested was the "most likely timing in US minds for military action to begin," came and went, and the inspectors went on searching.

On the Security Council, a majority—led by France, Germany, and Russia—pushed for the inspections to run their course. President Jacques Chirac of France later put this argument succinctly in an interview with CBS and CNN just as the war was about to begin:

> France is not pacifist. We are not anti-American either. We are not just going to use our veto to nag and annoy the US. But we just feel that there is another option, another way, another more normal way, a less dramatic way than war, and that we have to go through that path. And we should pursue it until we've come [to] a dead end, but that isn't [yet] the case.[6]

---

6. See "Chirac Makes His Case on Iraq," an interview with Christiane Amanpour, CBS News, March 16, 2003.

Where would this "dead end" be found, however, and who would determine that it had been found? Would it be the French, or the Americans? The logical flaw that threatened the administration's policy now began to become clear. Had the inspectors found weapons, or had they been presented with them by Saddam Hussein, many who had supported the resolution would argue that the inspections regime it established had indeed begun to work—that by multilateral action the world was succeeding, peacefully, in "disarming Iraq." As long as the inspectors found no weapons, however, many would argue that the inspectors "must be given time to do their work" —until, in Chirac's words, they "came to a dead end." However that point might be determined, it is likely that, long before it was reached, the failure to find weapons would have undermined the administration's central argument for going to war—"the conjunction," as "C" had put it that morning in July, "of terrorism and WMD." And as we now know, the inspectors would never have found weapons of mass destruction.

Vice President Cheney had anticipated this problem, as he had explained frankly to Hans Blix, the chief UN weapons inspector, during an October 30 meeting in the White House. Cheney, according to Blix, stated the position that inspections, if they do not give results, cannot go on forever, and said the US was "ready to discredit inspections in favor of disarmament." A pretty straight way, I thought, of saying that if we did not soon find the weapons of mass destruction that the US was convinced Iraq possessed (though they did not know where), the US would be ready to say that the inspectors were useless and embark on disarmament by other means.[7]

Indeed, the inspectors' failure to find any evidence of weapons came in the wake of a very large effort launched by the administration to put before the world evidence of Saddam's arsenal, an effort spearheaded by George W. Bush's speech in Cincinnati on October 7, and followed by a series of increasingly lurid disclosures to the press that reached a crescendo with Colin Powell's multimedia presentation to the UN Security Council on February 5, 2003. Throughout the fall and winter, the administration had "introduced the new product," in Card's phrase, with great skill, making use of television, radio, and all the print press to get its message out about the imminent threat

---

7. See Hans Blix, *Disarming Iraq* (Pantheon, 2004), p. 86.

of Saddam's arsenal. ("Think of the press," as Joseph Goebbels had advised, "as a great keyboard on which the government can play.")

As the gap between administration rhetoric about enormous arsenals—"we know where they are," asserted Donald Rumsfeld—and the inspectors' empty hands grew wider, that gap, as Cheney had predicted, had the effect in many quarters of undermining the credibility of the United Nations process itself. The inspectors' failure to find weapons in Iraq was taken to discredit the worth of the inspections, rather than to cast doubt on the administration's contention that Saddam possessed large stockpiles of weapons of mass destruction.

Oddly enough, Saddam's only effective strategy to prevent war at this point might have been to reveal and yield up some weapons, thus demonstrating to the world that the inspections were working. As we now know, however, he had no weapons to yield up. As Blix remarks, "It occurred to me [on March 7] that the Iraqis would be in greater difficulty if…there truly were no weapons of which they could 'yield possession.'" The fact that, in Blix's words, "the UN and the world had succeeded in disarming Iraq without knowing it"—that the UN process had been successful—meant, in effect, that the inspectors would be discredited and the United States would go to war.

President Bush would do so, of course, having failed to get the "second resolution" so desired by his friend and ally, Tony Blair. Blair had predicted, that July morning on Downing Street, that the "two key issues were whether the military plan worked and whether we had the political strategy to give the military plan the space to work." He seems to have been proved right in this. In the end his political strategy only half worked: the Security Council's refusal to vote a second resolution approving the use of force left "the UN route" discussed that day incomplete, and Blair found himself forced to follow the United States without the protection of international approval. Had the military plan "worked"—had the war been short and decisive rather than long, bloody, and inconclusive—Blair would perhaps have escaped the political damage the war has caused him. A week after the Downing Street memo was published in the *Sunday Times*, Tony Blair was reelected, but his majority in Parliament was reduced, from 161 to 67. The Iraq war, and the damage it had done to his reputation for probity, was widely believed to have been a principal cause.

In the United States, on the other hand, the Downing Street memorandum has attracted little attention. As I write, no American newspaper has published it and few writers have bothered to comment on it. The war continues, and Americans have grown weary of it; few seem much interested now in discussing how it began, and why their country came to fight a war in the cause of destroying weapons that turned out not to exist. For those who want answers, the Bush administration has followed a simple and heretofore largely successful policy: blame the intelligence agencies. Since "the intelligence and facts were being fixed around the policy" as early as July 2002 (as "C," the head of British intelligence, reported upon his return from Washington), it seems a matter of remarkable hubris, even for this administration, that its officials now explain their misjudgments in going to war by blaming them on "intelligence failures"—that is, on the intelligence that they themselves politicized. Still, for the most part, Congress has cooperated. Though the Senate Intelligence Committee investigated the failures of the CIA and other agencies before the war, a promised second report that was to take up the administration's political use of intelligence—which is, after all, the critical issue—was postponed until after the 2004 elections, then quietly abandoned.

In the end, the Downing Street memo, and Americans' lack of interest in what it shows, casts light upon a certain attitude about facts, or rather about where the line should be drawn between facts and political opinion. It calls to mind an interesting observation that an unnamed "senior advisor" to President Bush made to a *New York Times Magazine* reporter last fall:

> The aide said that guys like me [i.e., reporters and commentators] were "in what we call the reality-based community," which he defined as people who "believe that solutions emerge from your judicious study of discernible reality." I nodded and murmured something about enlightenment principles and empiricism. He cut me off. "That's not the way the world really works anymore," he continued. "We're an empire now, and when we act, we create our own reality. And while you're studying that reality—judiciously, as you will—we'll act again, creating other new realities, which you can study too, and that's how things will sort out. We're history's actors . . . and you, all of you, will be left to just study what we do."[8]

Power, so the argument runs, can shape truth: power, in the end, can determine reality, or at least the reality that most people

---

8. See Ron Suskind, "Without a Doubt," *The New York Times Magazine*, October 17, 2004.

accept—a critical point, for the administration has been singu-
larly effective in its recognition that what is most politically
important is not what readers of The New York Times believe but
what most Americans are willing to believe. The last century's
most innovative authority on power and truth, Joseph
Goebbels, made the same point but rather more directly:

> There was no point in seeking to convert the intellec-
> tuals. For intellectuals would never be converted and
> would anyway always yield to the stronger, and this
> will always be "the man in the street." Arguments
> must therefore be crude, clear and forcible, and appeal
> to emotions and instincts, not the intellect. Truth was
> unimportant and entirely subordinate to tactics and
> psychology.[9]

I thought of this quotation when I first read the Downing
Street memorandum; but I had first looked it up several
months earlier, on December 14, 2004, after I had seen the

---

9. This paragraph, though widely quoted as solely the words of Goebbels himself. is in fact an amalgam of Goebbels and the quite precise paraphrase of his
editor, Hugh Trevor-Roper. See Hugh Trevor-Roper, "Introduction" to Final Entries
1945:The Goebbels Diaries (Putnam, 1978), p. 20. [footnote added]

images of the newly reelected President George W. Bush award-
ing the Medal of Freedom, the highest civilian honor the
United States can bestow, to George Tenet, the former director
of central intelligence; L. Paul Bremer, the former head of the
Coalition Provisional Authority in Iraq; and General (ret.)
Tommy Franks, the commander who had led American forces
during the first phase of the Iraq war. Tenet, of course, would
be known to history as the intelligence director who had failed
to detect and prevent the attacks of September 11 and the man
who had assured President Bush that the case for Saddam's possession of weapons of mass destruction was "a slam dunk."
Franks had allowed the looting of Baghdad and had generally
done little to prepare for what would come after the occupation of Iraq. ("There was little discussion in Washington," as
"C" told the prime minister on July 23, "of the aftermath after
military action.") Bremer had dissolved the Iraqi army and the
Iraqi police and thereby created 400,000 or so available
recruits for the insurgency. One might debate their ultimate
responsibility for these grave errors, but it is difficult to argue
that these officials merited the highest recognition the country
could offer.

Of course truth, as the master propagandist believed, is "unim-
portant and entirely subordinate to tactics and psychology." He

of course would have instantly grasped the psychological tactic embodied in that White House ceremony, which was one more effort to reassure Americans that the war the administration launched against Iraq has been a success and was worth fighting. That barely four Americans in ten are still willing to believe this suggests that as time goes on and the gap grows between what Americans see and what they are told, membership in the "reality-based community" may grow along with it. We will see. Still, for those interested in the question of how our leaders persuaded the country to become embroiled in a counterinsurgency war in Iraq, the Downing Street memorandum offers one more confirmation of the truth. For those, that is, who want to hear.

—May 12, 2005

As published in The New York Review of Books
July 14, 2005

WHY THE MEMO MATTERS

TO THE EDITORS:

Mark Danner's excellent article on the Bush administration's path to war in Iraq missed a couple of important signposts.

On October 11, 2001, Knight Ridder reported that less than a month after the September 11 attacks senior Pentagon officials who wanted to expand the war against terrorism to Iraq had authorized a trip to Great Britain in September by former CIA director James Woolsey in search of evidence that Saddam Hussein had played a role in the September 11 terrorist attacks.

Then, on February 13, 2002, nearly six months before the Downing Street memo was written, Knight Ridder reported that President Bush had decided to oust Saddam Hussein and had ordered the CIA, the Pentagon, and other agencies to devise a combination of military, diplomatic, and covert steps to achieve that goal. Six days later, former Senator Bob Graham of Florida reports in his book, he was astounded when General Tommy Franks told him during a visit to the US Central Command in Tampa that the administration was shifting resources away from the pursuit of al-Qaeda in Afghanistan and Pakistan to prepare for war in Iraq.

JOHN WALCOTT

Washington Bureau Chief
Knight Ridder

MARK DANNER REPLIES:

John Walcott is proud of his bureau's reporting, and he should be. As my colleague Michael Massing has written in these pages, during the lead-up to the Iraq war Knight Ridder reporters had an enviable and unexampled record of independence and success.[1] But Mr. Walcott's statement that in my article "The Secret Way to War" I "missed a couple of important signposts" brings up an obvious question: Signposts on the way to what? What exactly does the Downing Street memo (which is simply an official account of a British security cabinet meeting in July 2002), and related documents that have since appeared, prove? And why has the American press in large part still resisted acknowledging the story the documents tell?

As I wrote in my article,

> The great value of the discussion recounted in the memo...is to show, for the governments of both countries, a clear hierarchy of decision-making. By July 2002 at the latest, war had been decided on; the question at issue now was how to justify it—how to "fix," as it were, what Blair will later call "the political

---

1. See Michael Massing, "Now They Tell Us," *The New York Review*, February 26, 2004.

context." Specifically, though by this point in July the President had decided to go to war, he had not yet decided to go to the United Nations and demand inspectors; indeed, as "C" [the chief of MI6, the British equivalent of the CIA] points out, those on the National Security Council—the senior security officials of the US government—"had no patience with the UN route, and no enthusiasm for publishing material on the Iraqi regime's record." This would later change, largely as a result of the political concerns of these very people gathered together at 10 Downing Street.

Those "political concerns" centered on the fact that, as British Foreign Secretary Jack Straw points out, "the case [for going to war] was thin" since, as the attorney general points out, "the desire for regime change [in Iraq] was not a legal base for military action." In order to secure such a legal base, the British officials agree, the allies must contrive to win the approval of the United Nations Security Council, and the foreign secretary puts forward a way to do that: "We should work up a plan for an ultimatum to Saddam to allow back in the UN weapons inspectors." Prime Minister Tony Blair makes very clear the point of such an ultimatum: "It would make a big difference politically and legally if Saddam refused to allow in the inspectors."

On February 13, 2002—five months before this British Cabinet meeting, and thirteen months before the war began—the second of the articles Mr. Walcott mentions had appeared, under his and Walter P. Strobel's byline and the stark headline "Bush Has Decided to Overthrow Hussein." The article concludes this way:

> Many nations...can be expected to question the legality of the United States unilaterally removing another country's government, no matter how distasteful. But a senior State Department official, while unable to provide the precise legal authority for such a move, said, "It's not hard to make the case that Iraq is a threat to international peace and security."...
>
> A diplomatic offensive aimed at generating international support for overthrowing Saddam's regime is likely to precede any attack on Iraq....
>
> The United States, perhaps with UN backing, is then expected to demand that Saddam readmit inspectors to root out Iraq's chemical, biological, nuclear and missile programs....

> If Baghdad refuses to readmit inspectors or if Saddam
> prevents them from carrying out their work, as he has
> in the past, Bush would have a pretext for action.

Thus the stratagem that the British would successfully urge on their American allies by late that summer was already under discussion within the State Department—five months before the Downing Street meeting in July 2002, and more than a year before the war began.

Again, what does all this prove? From the point of view of "the senior State Department official," no doubt, such an admission leaked to a Knight Ridder reporter was an opening public salvo in the bureaucratic struggle that reached a climax that August, when President Bush finally accepted the argument of his secretary of state, and his British allies, and went "the United Nations route." Just in the way that unnoticed but prophetic intelligence concealed in a wealth of "chatter" is outlined brightly by future events, this leak now seems like a clear prophetic disclosure about what was to come, having been confirmed by what did in fact happen. But the Downing Street memo makes clear that at the time the "senior State Department official" spoke to the Knight Ridder reporters the strategy had not yet been decided. The memo, moreover, is not an anonymous statement to reporters but a record of what Britain's highest security officials actually said. It tells us much about how the decision was made, and shows decisively that, as I wrote in my article, "the idea of UN inspectors was introduced not as a means to avoid war, as President Bush repeatedly assured Americans, but as a means to make war possible."

The Knight Ridder pieces bring up a larger issue. It is a source of some irony that one of the obstacles to gaining recognition for the Downing Street memo in the American press has been the largely unspoken notion among reporters and editors that the story the memo tells is "nothing new." I say irony because we see in this an odd and familiar narrative from our current world of "frozen scandal"—so-called scandals, that is, in which we have revelation but not a true investigation or punishment: scandals we are forced to live with.[2] A story is told the first time but hardly acknowledged (as with the Knight Ridder piece), largely because the broader story the government is telling drowns it out. When the story is later confirmed by official documents, in this case the Downing Street memorandum, the documents are largely dismissed because they contain "nothing new."

2. See my essay "What Are You Going To Do With That?," The New York Review, June 23, 2005.

Part of this comes down to the question of what, in our current political and journalistic world, constitutes a "fact." How do we actually prove the truth of a story, such as the rather obvious one that, as the Knight Ridder headline had it, "Bush has decided to overthrow Hussein" many months before the war and the congressional resolution authorizing it, despite the President's protestations that "no decision had been made"? How would one prove the truth of the story that fully eight months before the invasion of Iraq, as the head of British intelligence reports to his prime minister and his Cabinet colleagues upon his return from Washington in July 2002, "the facts and the intelligence were being fixed around the policy"? Michael Kinsley, in a recent article largely dismissing the Downing Street memo, remarks about this sentence:

> Of course, if "intelligence and facts were being fixed around the policy," rather than vice versa, that is pretty good evidence of Bush's intentions, as well as a scandal in its own right. And we know now that was true and a half. Fixing intelligence and facts to fit a desired policy is the Bush II governing style, especially concerning the war in Iraq. But C offered no specifics, or none that made it into the memo. Nor

does the memo assert that actual decision makers had told him they were fixing the facts.[3]

Consider for a moment this paragraph, which strikes me as a perfect little poem on our current political and journalistic state. Kinsley accepts as "true and a half" that "the intelligence and facts were being fixed around the policy"—that is, after all, "the Bush II governing style"—but rejects the notion that the Downing Street memo actually proves this, since, presumably, the head of British intelligence "does [not] assert that actual decision makers had told him they were fixing the facts." Kinsley does not say from whom he thinks the chief of British intelligence, in reporting to his prime minister "on his recent talks in Washington," might have derived that information, if not "actual decision makers." (In fact, as the London *Sunday Times* reported, among the people he saw was his American counterpart, director of central intelligence George Tenet.) Kinsley does say that if the point, which he accepts as true— indeed, almost blithely dismissing all who might doubt it— could in fact be proved, it would be "pretty good evidence of Bush's intentions, as well as a scandal in its own right."

---

3. *The Washington Post*, August 12, 2005.

One might ask what would convince this writer, and many others, of the truth of what, apparently, they already know, and accept, and acknowledge that they know and accept. What could be said to establish "truth"—to "prove it"? Perhaps a true congressional investigation of the way the administration used intelligence before the war—an investigation of the kind that, as I wrote in my article, was promised by the Senate Intelligence Committee, then thoughtfully postponed until after the election—though one might think the question might have had some relevance to Americans in deciding for whom to vote—then finally, and quietly, abandoned. Instead, the Senate committee produced a report that, while powerfully damning on its own terms, explicitly excluded the critical question of how administration officials made use of the intelligence that was supplied them.

Still, Kinsley's column, and the cynical and impotent attitude it represents, suggests that such an investigation, if it occurred, might still not be adequate to make a publicly acceptable fact out of what everyone now knows and accepts. The column bears the perfect headline "No Smoking Gun," which suggests that failing the discovery of a tape recording in which President Bush is quoted explicitly ordering then Director of Central Intelligence George Tenet that he should "fix the intelligence and facts around the policy," many will never regard the case as proved—though all the while accepting, of course, and admitting that they accept, that this is indeed what happened. The so-called "rules of objective journalism" dovetail with the disciplined functioning of a one-party government to keep the political debate willfully stupid and opaque.

So: if the excellent Knight Ridder articles by Mr. Walcott and his colleagues do indeed represent "signposts," then signposts on the way to what? American citizens find themselves on a very peculiar road, stumbling blindly through a dark wood. Having had before the war rather clear evidence that the Bush administration had decided to go to war even as it was claiming it was trying to avert war, we are now confronted with an escalating series of "disclosures" proving that the original story, despite the broad unwillingness to accept it, was in fact true.

Many in Congress now find themselves in an especially difficult position. These congressmen and senators—among them many leading Democrats who voted to give the President the authority to go to war, fearing the political consequences of opposing him and opposing what might have been a popular war, and thus welcomed his soothing arguments that such a vote would enable him to avoid war rather than to undertake it—now claim that they were "misled" into supporting a war that they believed they were voting to help prevent. (Senator Kerry made this claim a centerpiece of his presidential campaign.) For them to have plausibly believed this, however, the administration's original argument must have had at least some degree of credibility. In fact, as the Downing Street memo reminds us, that argument was embarrassingly thin. The prowar Democrats' argument is morally incriminating enough to go on confusing and corrupting a public debate on Iraq that is sure to become more difficult and painful.

Whether or not the Downing Street memo could be called a "smoking gun," it has long since become clear that the UN inspections policy that, given time, could in fact have prevented war—by revealing, as it eventually would have, that Saddam had no threatening stockpiles of "weapons of mass destruction"—was used by the administration as a pretext: a means to persuade the country to begin a war that need never have been fought. It was an exceedingly clever pretext, for every action preparing for war could by definition be construed to be an action intended to avert it—as necessary to convince Saddam that war was imminent. According to this rhetorical stratagem, the actions, whether preparing to wage war or seeking to avert it, merge, become indistinguishable. Failing the emergence of a time-stamped recording of President Bush declaring, "I have today decided to go to war with Saddam and all this inspection stuff is rubbish," we are unlikely to recover the kind of "smoking gun" that Kinsley and others seem to demand.

Failing that, the most reliable way to distinguish the true intentions of Bush and his officials is by looking at what they actually did, and the fact is that, despite the protestations of many in the United Nations and throughout the world, they refused to let the inspections run their course. What is more, the arguments that the President and others in his administration have put forward retrospectively justifying the war after the failure to find weapons of mass destruction in Iraq—stressing that Saddam would always have been a threat because he could have "reconstituted" his weapons programs—make a mockery of the proposition that the administration would have been willing to leave him in power, even if the inspectors had been allowed sufficient time to prove before the war, as their colleagues did after it, that no weapons existed in Iraq.

We might believe that we are past such matters now. Alas, as Americans go on dying in Iraq and their fellow citizens grow ever more impatient with the war, the story of its beginning, clouded with propaganda and controversy as it is, will become more important, not less. Consider the strong warning put forward in a recently released British Cabinet document dated two days before the Downing Street memo (and eight months before the war), that "the military occupation of Iraq could lead to a protracted and costly nation-building exercise." On this point, as the British document prophetically observes, "US military plans are virtually silent."[4] So too were America's leaders, and we live with the consequences of that silence.

---

4. See the Cabinet Office paper "Iraq: Conditions for Military Action," pp. 150–163, below.

THE MEMO, THE PRESS, AND THE WAR

In "Why the Memo Matters," Mark Danner commented on a *Washington Post* column by Michael Kinsley, "No Smoking Gun," published on June 12, 2005 (see pages 37–41). The following exchange was published in *The New York Review of Books* of August 11, 2005

TO THE EDITORS:

It's easy to appreciate the frustration of "Downing Street Memo" enthusiasts like Mark Danner. They think they have documentary proof that President Bush had firmly decided to go to war against Iraq by July 2002. Yet some people say the memo isn't newsworthy because the charge is not true, while others say the memo isn't newsworthy because the charge is so obviously true. A smoking gun is sitting there on the table, but he's going to get away with murder because everyone—for different reasons—won't pick it up.

And I think Danner is right to resent the whole "smoking gun" business—an artifact of Watergate—which comes close to establishing the old Chico Marx joke, "Who are you gonna believe: me or your own two eyes," as a serious standard of proof. Not every villain is going to tape record his villainy. George W. Bush, as I noted in the column that Danner objects to, is especially good at insisting that reality is what he would like it to be, and the smoking-gun standard helps him to get away with this.

But the DSM is worthless if it is not a smoking gun—not because I need a smoking gun to be persuaded (a "cynical and impotent attitude," Danner says), but precisely because people who don't require a smoking gun are already persuaded. And the document is just not that smoking gun. It basically says that the conventional wisdom in Washington in July 2002 was that Bush had made up his mind and war was certain. "What," Danner asks, "could be said to establish 'truth'—to 'prove it'?" I suggested in the column that it would have been nice if the memo had made clear that the people saying facts were fixed and war was certain were actual administration decision-makers. Danner asks, Who else could the head of British intelligence, reporting on the mood and gossip of "Washington," be talking about if not "actual decision-makers"? He has got to be kidding.

In short, the DSM will not persuade anyone who is not already persuaded. That doesn't make it wrong. But that does make the memo fairly worthless.

MICHAEL KINSLEY

Los Angeles Times

MARK DANNER REPLIES:

For more than two years the United States has been fighting a war in Iraq that was launched in the cause of destroying weapons that turned out not to exist. One might have thought such a strange and unprecedented historical event—which has thus far cost the lives of nearly eighteen hundred young Americans, and counting—might attract the strong and sustained interest of a free press. It has—in Great Britain. In the United States when it comes to this central issue of our politics we have in general been treated to the vaguely depressing spectacle of a great many very intelligent people struggling very hard to make themselves stupid. Such has been the general plot line of the press reception of the so-called Downing Street memo and the other government documents associated with it, which tell much about how the Iraq war actually began. I'm afraid the admirable Michael Kinsley, in dismissing the memo as "worthless" (he later promotes it to "fairly worthless"), once again rather exemplifies this trend.

Though leaders in the United Kingdom and the United States have tried hard to cast the memo as something exotic and recondite—"people...take bits out here of this memo or that memo, or something someone's supposed to have said at the time," as Prime Minister Tony Blair put it in Washington last month[1]—in fact the document is nothing more than the record of a meeting Blair had with his highest officials at 10 Downing Street on July 23, 2002. Despite Blair's dismissal of the memo, no one, including him, has suggested that the

---

1. In an interview with Gwen Ifill on *The NewsHour with Jim Lehrer*, June 7, 2005.

minutes of the meeting—the equivalent of a National Security Council meeting in the United States—are anything but genuine. The Downing Street memo is an actual record of what Britain's highest officials were saying, in private, about the coming Iraq war eight months before the war started.

The meeting began—as indeed most National Security Council meetings begin—with a summary of the current intelligence. Sir Richard Dearlove, the head of MI6, Britain's equivalent of the CIA, had just returned from high-level consultations in the United States. To begin the discussion, then, Sir Richard "reported on his recent talks in Washington." Here once again, in its entirety, is the report Sir Richard gave to his prime minister and his colleagues:

> There was a perceptible shift in attitude. Military action was now seen as inevitable. Bush wanted to remove Saddam, through military action, justified by the conjunction of terrorism and WMD. But the intelligence and facts were being fixed around the policy. The NSC had no patience with the UN route, and no enthusiasm for publishing material on the Iraqi regime's record. There was little discussion in Washington of the aftermath after military action.

Mr. Kinsley contends that here Sir Richard is reporting on "the mood and gossip of 'Washington'"—as opposed, he says, to the views of "actual administration decision-makers." I am unsure whom Kinsley thinks the head of British intelligence sees when he takes a secret trip to Washington to consult with his country's most important ally about a coming war. We know Sir Richard met with Director of Central Intelligence George Tenet, his opposite number, who, as a Cabinet member who briefs the President personally every morning, would presumably be considered an "actual administration decision-maker." We can assume that the other calls that the head of British intelligence paid during his "talks in Washington" were at a comparably high level.[2]

Of course, none of Sir Richard's colleagues, including his prime minister, demand to know who his sources were. And yet they go forward with the meeting, taking Sir Richard's central points—that war is inevitable, that intelligence is being fixed to prepare for it and for a "justification" based on "the conjunction of terrorism and WMD," and that the United States will resist going "the UN route"—as the point of departure, setting off a discussion (the true heart of the memo) of the need to persuade the United States to "go the UN route" to

---

2. For more on Sir Richard's visit to Washington, see the Afterword, pp. 71–74.

give some clothing of legality to a war the legal case for which, as the foreign secretary says, is quite "thin." Why is it, one might ask, that the prime minister and the highest security officials of Great Britain do not demand that Sir Richard reveal his sources—why is it, in other words, that these officials are so much more credulous than Michael Kinsley?

Could it be because the prime minister and other officials think Sir Richard on his return from Washington is bringing from officials at the highest levels of the American government ("actual administration decision-makers") information of the highest reliability—information, no doubt, that echoes what the Cabinet ministers themselves have been hearing from their own Washington opposite numbers?

Indeed, if, as Mr. Kinsley contends, what Sir Richard tells his prime minister and his colleagues represents not the views of "actual administration decision-makers" but the "mood and gossip of 'Washington,'" then does it not seem rather odd that the highest officials of Great Britain, America's closest ally, would rely on it to make their own most vital decisions of national security? Does it not seem rather more plausible to believe what Prime Minister Blair and his ministers all seem to believe: that what Sir Richard says in his report represents the definitive views of "actual administration decision-makers" and not the speculations of journalists or cab drivers? As Michael Smith, the London *Times* reporter—and strong Iraq war supporter—who first published this document, said when asked about the authority and sources of Sir Richard Dearlove:

> This was the head of MI6. How much authority do you want the man to have? He has just been to Washington, he has just talked to George Tenet. He said the intelligence and facts were being fixed around the policy. That translates in clearer terms as the intelligence was being cooked to match what the administration wanted it to say to justify invading Iraq. Fixed means the same here as it does there.[3]

Who—in Kinsley's phrase—has got to be kidding?

There is, of course, the further point, not a minor one, that pretty much everything Sir Richard says in his little summary turns out to be true. America and Britain did go to war to remove Saddam. Military action was justified by the conjunction of terrorism and WMD. The US did have no idea what to

---

3. See "The Downing Street Memo" and the interview with Michael Smith, *Washington Post* online, www.washingtonpost.com/wpdyn/content/discussion/2005/06/14/DI2005061401261_pf.html.

do in "the aftermath after military action." And the intelligence and facts were fixed around the policy.

Of course, according to the rules under which Kinsley, and much of the rest of the American press, profess to be playing, one cannot say this; after all, this is the case that the Downing Street memo, all by itself, must be shown to prove. But the requirement is purely artificial. Though, scandalously, the country has had no properly constituted investigation, congressional or otherwise, empowered to look into policymakers' use of intelligence before the Iraq war—indeed, such investigations as there have been have explicitly excluded precisely this central issue[4]—an avalanche of other proof has shown how the administration "fixed the facts" around its policy of invading Iraq.

It is plain by now that the intelligence the CIA and other US agencies produced on Iraq and its weapons programs was poor,

---

4. For example, the Commission on the Intelligence Capabilities of the United States Regarding Weapons of Mass Destruction, commonly known as the Robb-Silberman Commission, notes that the executive order which established it "did not authorize us to investigate how policymakers used the intelligence they received from the Intelligence Community on Iraq's weapons programs." This prohibition, also included in the Republican-controlled Senate Intelligence Committee's report, derived, as the *Times* remarked on the report's release, "from the mandate [the President] gave it more than a year ago, when the White House feared the issue could affect the election." See Scott Shane and David Sanger, "Bush Panel Finds Big Flaws Remain in US Spy Efforts," *The New York Times*, April 1, 2005.

and was built on shockingly shallow information. It is also plain that Bush administration officials, far from pressing the agencies for the best, most reliable intelligence, instead relentlessly and blatantly exaggerated the slender intelligence that the government did possess, in order to make its case for war. Though thus far the administration has managed to block a true investigation of this misuse of intelligence by policymakers, and the Republican-controlled Congress has gone along, many examples of it are already known to the public.

One could cite President Bush's insistence on telling the world that "Saddam Hussein recently sought significant quantities of uranium from Africa," when the CIA had explicitly warned him that it could not confirm this information. One could point to the administration's doctoring of the declassified version of the National Intelligence Estimate on Iraq given to Congress in October 2002, in which all of the considerable qualifiers included in the original report were removed. One could quote the repeated references by Vice President Cheney, Condoleezza Rice, and other officials to "reconstituted nuclear weapons" and a "smoking gun becoming a mushroom cloud," when the administration had little or no real evidence to prove Iraq had an ongoing nuclear program.

The fact is that the administration blatantly exaggerated the intelligence it was given to convince the country to go to war—

"introducing the new product," as White House Chief of Staff Andrew Card called the coming public relations campaign in August 2002—and then, after the fall of Baghdad, when the weapons of mass destruction refused to turn up, the President and other administration officials blamed the CIA and other agencies for supplying intelligence that was "misleading." Having politicized the intelligence before the war, administration officials turned around and blamed the intelligence agencies for misleading them—with the very intelligence that they themselves had politicized.

That the Republican Congress—and notably the Senate Intelligence Committee—has failed to fully investigate this is not news; as I wrote in my article, the committee first separated the question of "policymakers' use of intelligence" from the question of the performance of the intelligence agencies themselves, then helpfully postponed its investigation of the first question —the critical question—until after the election; now the promised report has been abandoned altogether. Still, the administration's "fixing of the facts and intelligence around the policy" has been quite well documented in other, public sources.[5]

5. See, for publicly available documents, the excellent early report, "WMD in Iraq: Evidence and Implications" (Carnegie Endowment for International Peace, 2003), and also John Prados, *Hoodwinked: The Documents That Reveal How Bush Sold Us a War* (New Press, 2004).

Indeed, one catches glimpses of it even in the severely circumscribed reports that Congress and the administration have allowed to be produced.[6] That is, if anyone still needs to be convinced; as Kinsley writes in his original column, "we know now that was true and a half. Fixing intelligence and facts to fit a desired policy is the Bush II governing style, especially concerning the war in Iraq."

If Kinsley is convinced that it is "true and a half" that the Bush "governing style, especially concerning the war in Iraq," is to "fix intelligence and facts to fit a desired policy," then what exactly was the evidence that convinced him? On this point he is silent. Presumably he has gained this conviction after reading various accounts of the decision-making leading up to the war, notably Bob Woodward's and Richard Clarke's; after examining certain documents, such as those I have cited; and after watching the progress of events during the last several years. Presumably the Downing Street memo would bolster

---

6. Even the Robb-Silberman report notes, in the words of an unidentified national intelligence officer (or NIO), "a 'zeitgeist' or general 'climate' of policymaker focus on Iraq's WMD that permeated the analytical atmosphere" and "was formed in part, the NIO claimed, by the gathering conviction among analysts that war with Iraq was inevitable. . . ." Elsewhere the commissioners conceded that "it is hard to deny the conclusion that intelligence analysts worked in an environment that did not encourage skepticism about the conventional wisdom." See the Report of the Commission on the Intelligence Capabilities of the United States Regarding Weapons of Mass Destruction, pp. 190 and 11.

these conclusions by shoring up the various secondhand and other sources with the actual recorded words of "actual decision-makers" who are discussing the decisions themselves during the months preceding the war. By insisting on applying an artificially and narrowly legalistic standard to the Downing Street memo, Kinsley discards as "worthless" a higher order of historical evidence than has yet been made public. To reduce serious analysis to a legalistic game in this way impoverishes the attempt to chronicle the real history of a war in which Americans, and Iraqis, are still dying. It means, in effect, deliberately blindfolding ourselves.

We come by information incrementally, and give it sense by placing it in a context we have already constructed; that is why Kinsley's "test" for whether or not the Downing Street memo is "worthless" is so misguided. Those who do look at the memo's account of the Cabinet meeting with some honesty—and I urge readers to go to the memo itself; it is barely three pages long and The New York Review has published it in full[7]—will find it confirms a precise historical narrative of the run-up to the war. It is clearly written and, notwithstanding the comments of Kinsley and others, unambiguous.

7. See pages 87–93, below. The text can also be found widely online, including at downingstreetmemo.com.

What is most deadening and in the end saddening about Kinsley's letter and earlier article is the attitude they exemplify toward history; we see here a deliberate impoverishment, a turning of inquiry and, at bottom, of curiosity into a dull and sterile game of black and white, played by rules that fail to reflect what anyone actually believes. Such rules dovetail perfectly with the grim and gray shutting down of information elsewhere in the Republic, as evidenced most prominently by the Republican-controlled Congress, which, having endorsed a war in the name of destroying weapons that turned out not to exist, has responded by forbidding any thorough investigation into precisely how such a strange set of events could come to pass. Kinsley, like many others in the American press, wants to judge the memo's "worth" on whether or not it contains, as he says, "documentary proof that President Bush had firmly decided to go to war against Iraq by July 2002." As I have written, such "documentary proof"—if we are talking about firm and incontrovertible evidence of what was in Mr. Bush's mind at the time—is destined to prove elusive; the President can always claim, all appearances and outward evidence to the contrary, that he "hadn't made up his mind." And so he has claimed.

The fact is that this is not what is most important about the memo and about the documents that have accompanied it. What the memo clearly shows is that the decision to "go to the United Nations" was in large part a response to the British concern that "the legal case for war" was "thin," in the words of British Foreign Secretary Jack Straw. In other words, securing the blessing of the United Nations Security Council was thought to be the only way to give the war a legal clothing. It is worth quoting this passage in full, for Straw puts the matter with admirable concision:

> It seemed clear that Bush had made up his mind to take military action, even if the timing was not yet decided. But the case was thin. Saddam was not threatening his neighbours, and his WMD capability was less than that of Libya, North Korea or Iran. We should work up a plan for an ultimatum to Saddam to allow back in the UN weapons inspectors. This would also help with the legal justification for the use of force.

The original idea of "the UN route," as set out by the foreign secretary and prime minister, was to issue an ultimatum to Saddam that he allow into Iraq a new team of UN inspectors and then, when he refused the ultimatum, to use his refusal as a justification to invade the country under Security Council mandate. It "would make a big difference politically and legally," as Prime Minister Tony Blair observes in the meeting, "if Saddam refused to allow in the UN inspectors." What the memo made clear, as I wrote, is that "the inspectors were introduced not as a means to avoid war, as President Bush repeatedly assured Americans, but as a means to make war possible."

On these matters Mr. Kinsley says nothing, either in his original article or in his letter, because he is concerned only with a single question: Does the memo offer "documentary proof that President Bush had firmly decided to go to war against Iraq by July 2002"? Having decided that the memo falls short of passing this stern test, he deems the document "worthless." Like many in the American press, he is so obsessed with finding the "smoking gun" that he pretty much manages to miss the point of what is in front of him.

In the event, of course, Saddam Hussein did not, as was hoped, reject the inspectors out of hand. He admitted them, and President Bush and Prime Minister Blair found themselves forced to demand their withdrawal—against the wishes of the Security Council and before they had completed their task—in order to begin the invasion of Iraq. The UN route, as it turned out, was messy; it meant arguing publicly with Hans Blix and other UN officials, fighting for and ultimately failing to secure a second Security Council resolution that would have blessed an invasion of Iraq, and finally withdrawing the inspectors when they had examined barely one hundred of the six hundred or so suspect sites—leaving the inspections to be concluded only after the fall of Baghdad, when the American Iraqi Survey Group finally ascertained what the UN team might have concluded before the war: that Saddam had destroyed his weapons of mass destruction long before.

Of course, in retrospect, the plot line would have been much "cleaner" if Saddam had obliged the British and the Americans by refusing to allow in the inspectors in the first place, as Prime Minister Tony Blair had hoped he would. President Bush had clearly hoped the same thing; indeed, in absent moments, he apparently goes on hoping it. Several months after the fall of Baghdad, sitting beside UN Secretary General Kofi Annan in the Oval Office, the President offered this version of his pre-war policy toward Saddam Hussein:

> We gave him a chance to allow the inspectors in,
> and he wouldn't let them in. And, therefore, after a

reasonable request, we decided to remove him from power.[8]

It seems unlikely that President Bush had failed to notice that Saddam had admitted the inspectors into his country. More plausibly, the President is simply making a slip of the tongue of the sort anyone could make—a slip prompted by a bit of wish fulfillment, with the President substituting what he and Tony Blair had wished would happen for what actually, in the event, did happen.

History is rich in this sort of thing, of course; understanding "what actually happened" is an ongoing task, demanding a constant reformulation of what we believe based on what we know. What is most dispiriting about the reception of the Downing Street memo and the other documents associated with it is the general willingness of reporters and commentators in this country to perform a complicated and willful act of shutting down their own minds and obliterating their own curiosity. Michael Smith, the London *Times* reporter, described the strange attitude of his American colleagues:

8. See "President Reaffirms Strong Position on Liberia," July 14, 2003, available at the White House Web site, www.whitehouse.gov/news/releases/2003/07/200302714-3.html.

There was a feeling of, "Well, we said that way back when." Then of course as the pressure mounted from the outside, there was a defensive attitude. "We have said this before, if you the reader didn't listen, well, what can we do." ...[But] it is one thing for The New York Times or The Washington Post to say that we were being told that the intelligence was being fixed by sources inside the CIA or Pentagon or the NSC and quite another to have documentary confirmation in the form of the minutes of a key meeting with the Prime Minister's office.

...This was the equivalent of an NSC meeting.... They say the evidence against Saddam Hussein is thin, the Brits think regime change is illegal under international law so we are going to have to go to the UN to get an ultimatum, not as a way of averting war but as an excuse to make the war legal.... Not reportable, are you kidding me?

A good deal of this "defensive attitude," certainly, as Smith implies, derives from the shortcomings of American reporting during the run-up to the war, when newspapers and broadcast stations showed very little skepticism about administration claims of Saddam's supposedly threatening arsenal of weapons of mass destruction.[9] Though in the months since, the country's most influential newspapers, including *The New York Times* and *The Washington Post*, in an unprecedented step, have explicitly apologized for their pre-war reporting, it is less clear that individual reporters feel that they made any mistakes, and many bristle at any implication that they did. The Downing Street memo serves, among other things, as a not very subtle reminder that much of the press was duped by the government in a rather premeditated and quite successful way. No one likes to be reminded of this, certainly not reporters and the institutions they work for; claiming the memo is "not reportable," in Smith's words, not only avoids revisiting a painful passage in American journalism but does so by asserting that the story "had already been covered"—that is, that it had never been missed in the first place. When it comes to the war, much of American journalism has little more institutional interest in reexamining the past than the Bush administration itself.

We must be grateful that the American polity is broader and more complex than the American press. Kinsley claims that the Downing Street memo

---

9. See Michael Massing, "Now They Tell Us," *The New York Review*, February 26, 2004.

will not persuade anyone who is not already persuaded. That doesn't make it wrong. But it does make
the memo fairly worthless.

But it is Kinsley who is quite demonstrably wrong on this
question. Whether or not the memo will "persuade anyone
who is not already persuaded" is of course an empirical question and I know myself a number of people who have been so
persuaded. And the fact that more than half of all Americans
now believe the President and his administration intentionally
"misled the American public before the war" seems a rather
strong suggestion that, as a matter of persuasion and of politics, the Downing Street memo is very far from worthless.[10]
The number of Americans who hold this view is likely to continue to grow. These are simply people who have begun to
notice the widening gap between what they are told and what
they see—a gap that, when it comes to the Iraq war, is becoming harder and harder to ignore. I would not call these people,
in Kinsley's phrase, "Downing Street memo enthusiasts." Better
to adopt a denigrating phrase from a Bush administration

---

10. The exact number is 52 percent, an increase of nine points in three months.
See The Washington Post/ABC poll, and the report by Richard Morin and Dan Baly,
"Survey Finds Most Support Staying in Iraq," The Washington Post, June 28, 2005.

adviser and dub them members of the "reality-based community." Their ranks are growing, and it may be that in the coming days some in the press will leave off the increasingly hard work of avoiding recent history and come and join them.

AFTERWORD

ON NOVEMBER 1, 2005, Senator Harry Reid, Democrat of Nevada and the minority leader, took to the Senate floor and delivered a blistering attack on the chamber's Republican leaders. He took as his point of departure the indictment, days before, of I. Lewis Libby Jr., chief of staff to the vice-president, which, Reid said,

> provides a window into... how the Administration manufactured and manipulated intelligence in order to sell the war in Iraq and attempted to destroy those who dared to challenge its actions.

Libby, the first sitting White House staff member to be indicted in more than a century, had been charged with misleading a grand jury and federal investigators about his involvement in publicly disclosing that Valerie Plame Wilson was a CIA officer. In 2002 the CIA had commissioned Plame's husband, former ambassador Joseph C. Wilson IV, to investigate allegations that Saddam Hussein's regime was attempting to buy uranium from Africa. After traveling to Niger, Wilson told the agency that the charges were baseless—and was thus surprised to hear President Bush in his State of the Union address in January 2003 utter those now infamous sixteen words: "The British government has learned that Saddam Hussein recently sought significant quantities of uranium from Africa." In early July 2003, even as the promised weapons of mass destruction were failing to turn up in occupied Iraq and shortly after Wilson described what he had not found in Africa in an article in *The New York Times*, administration officials apparently retaliated by leaking his wife's CIA connection.

Libby's behavior, Reid told the Senate, was part of a much broader pattern and thus exemplified how administration officials had "misstated and manipulated the facts" as they made the case for war:

> The American people were warned time and again by the President, the Vice President, and the current Secretary of State about Saddam's nuclear weapons capabilities. The Vice President said Iraq "has reconstituted its nuclear weapons." Playing upon the fears of Americans after September 11, these officials and others raised the specter that, left unchecked, Saddam could soon attack America with nuclear weapons. Obviously we know now their nuclear claims were wholly inaccurate. But more troubling is the fact that a lot of intelligence experts were telling the Administration then that its claims about Saddam's nuclear capabilities were false.

After discussing in detail the administration's "manipulation of intelligence," the Senate minority leader denounced the inaction of Congress:

> As a result of its improper conduct, a cloud now hangs over this Administration. [A] cloud also hangs over this Republican-controlled Congress for its unwillingness to hold this Republican Administration accountable for its misdeeds.... What has been the response of this Republican-controlled Congress to the Administration's manipulation of intelligence that led to this protracted war in Iraq? Basically nothing. Did the Republican-controlled Congress carry out its constitutional obligations to conduct oversight? No. Did it support our troops and their families by providing them the answers to many important questions? No. Did it even attempt to force this Administration to answer the most basic questions about its behavior? No.

Demanding that the intelligence committees "and other committees in this body...carry out a full and complete investigation immediately," Reid took the unusual and dramatic step of sending the Senate into closed session, there to discuss the long-promised report on policymakers' use of intelligence during the run-up to the Iraq war. The Democrats had seized the chance to shut down the Senate—for no votes could be taken or public business conducted while the chamber was in closed session—in order to call Americans' attention to the looming unanswered questions about how the war in Iraq began.

Reid's charges, of course, were familiar. Democrats' willingness to take aggressive action, however, was not. Reid was encouraged not only by Libby's indictment but by the President's approval ratings, which had been undermined by Americans' growing impatience with the war and by a widening suspicion that they had been misled about the reasons for it. But Reid's dramatic step brought no practical action in Congress. Nearly three years after the United States unleashed a war in Iraq, the Republican chairman of the Senate Intelligence Committee refused to offer a definite date for the delivery of his committee's long-promised report on the use of intelligence by policymakers during the run-up to the war.

Reid did well to focus in his Senate speech on the administration's claims about Saddam's "alleged nuclear weapons capabilities," for it was in conjuring before Americans the image of "the smoking gun" that would become "a mushroom cloud" that administration officials' exaggerations were most obvious and most calculated. Little if any evidence existed that Saddam had, in the words of Vice President Cheney, "reconstituted nuclear weapons," and authoritative bodies like the UN's International Atomic Energy Agency questioned—rightly, as it turned out—whether a program to develop nuclear weapons even existed in Iraq. When it came to chemical and biological weapons, however, the picture was more complicated. As the Downing Street documents make clear, British policymakers believed Saddam had them. "What were the consequences, if Saddam used WMD on day one" of the war? the chief of the Defence Staff asks near the end of the July 23 meeting. "Saddam could also use his WMD on Kuwait," Blair's foreign policy adviser warns. "Or on Israel," his defence secretary puts in. Though these officials acknowledge that "intelligence is poor" on Saddam's weapons programs, it seems plain that they believe that "Iraq continues to develop weapons of mass destruction" and that in the coming conflict Saddam will have those weapons at his disposal.

US officials, we must conclude, held similar beliefs. On July 20, 2002, three days before the meeting at 10 Downing Street, according to James Risen's account in his book *State of War* (which appeared just as this book was going to press), Sir

Richard Dearlove and other top MI6 officials had attended "a CIA–MI6 summit meeting held at CIA headquarters, in which the two sides had candid talks about both counterterrorism and Iraq." According to "a former senior CIA officer" Risen quotes, the all-day "summit meeting" was held "at the urgent request of the British."

> CIA officials believe that Prime Minister Blair had ordered Dearlove to go to Washington to find out what the Bush administration was really thinking about Iraq. While Blair was in constant communication with President Bush, he apparently wanted his intelligence chief to scout out the thinking of other senior officials in Washington, to give him a reality check on what he was hearing from the White House.
>
> "I think in hindsight that it is clear that Dearlove was insistent on having the summit because Blair wanted him to find out what was going on," said the former CIA official....
>
> The two sides ended up spending most of that Saturday [July 20] together.... Tenet had an especially good personal relationship with Dearlove. He was usually very candid with his British counterpart.

During the Saturday summit, Tenet and Dearlove left the larger meeting and went off by themselves for about an hour and a half, according to a former senior CIA official who attended the summit.[1]

So Sir Richard Dearlove's comments as recorded in the Downing Street memo, far from representing "the mood and gossip of 'Washington,'" actually bring together what the MI6 chief had learned in "a secret conference in Washington between top officials of the CIA and British intelligence" held specifically to give Blair "a reality check" on "what was going on" when it came to Iraq. And the real "back story" of the memo, says Risen, is the "acceptance of weak intelligence among senior CIA officials."

As the invasion of Iraq drew closer, an attitude took hold among many senior CIA officials that war was inevitable—and so the quality of the intelligence on weapons of mass destruction didn't really matter. This attitude led CIA management to cut corners and

---

1. See James Risen, *State of War: The Secret History of the CIA and the Bush Administration* (Free Press, 2006), pp. 113–115.

accept shoddy intelligence, other CIA officials believe. "One of the senior guys in the NE Division [the Near East Division of the Directorate of Operations] told me that it isn't going to matter once we go into Baghdad, we are going to find mountains of this stuff," recalled a former CIA official, who left the agency after the war.

This conclusion—that "the CIA chief and other CIA officials didn't believe that the WMD intelligence mattered, because war was coming one way or another"—is reflected in Dearlove's now famous words at 10 Downing Street three days after the Washington "summit": that "intelligence and facts were being fixed around the policy." While few of these officials may have doubted that the weapons were there, however poor the intelligence, they told themselves they could be careless about the specific intelligence because they knew what had long since become obvious: senior Bush administration officials were not carefully weighing intelligence on weapons of mass destruction to decide whether they constituted a threat that warranted launching a war to overthrow Saddam Hussein and occupy Iraq. Rather, they were making use of the intelligence as a tool in their "information campaign" to convince the public that it was vital for the United States to embark on a war that had long since been decided on.

When it came to the narrow issue of weapons of mass destruction and Iraq, the real question before the war was not whether or not Saddam Hussein possessed them; failing definitive proof that he had destroyed them, most intelligence agencies (wrongly, as it turned out) assumed that he did. The real question was whether those weapons, together with other facts about the regime, justified a war of choice to remove him—whether they constituted a great enough threat to the security of the United States to justify the risk of invading and occupying Iraq. To arrive at a real answer to that question would have meant weighing the intelligence (and its admitted weaknesses), assessing the state of the various Iraqi weapons programs and the threat they posed, and evaluating the strength and intentions of the Iraqi regime.

From what we know, administration officials, obsessed with "introducing their new product"—with selling the Iraq war to Americans and to the world—showed little interest in weighing the intelligence in this way but instead contented themselves with exaggerating what the intelligence agencies knew and making almost wholly unsupported allegations about Iraq's supposed "nuclear weapons capability." Administration officials knew that "the smoking gun becoming a nuclear cloud" was the nightmare image most likely to convince Americans to support a war, and to intimidate any politicians who might be inclined to express doubts about its wisdom. The administration's strategy, though, was built on the assumption that when American troops arrived in Iraq they would find at least some weapons of mass destruction—a stockpile of chemical artillery shells or a few biological weapons laboratories to put before the cameras. Had administration officials not sincerely believed that at least some weapons were there, it would have been imprudent at the least—however strong their conviction that the war would be a rapid and overwhelmingly popular success—to have based the entire propaganda strategy on their presence.

Of course, there is a difference between a reason and a pretext. It has long since become clear that officials of the Bush administration decided to invade and occupy Iraq for a number of reasons, some of which predated the September 11 attacks: to remove the threat a hostile and unpredictable dictator was thought to pose to the Persian Gulf and the industrial world's oil supply; to foreclose the possibility of any collaboration between Saddam and al-Qaeda (which might include the transfer of weapons of mass destruction); to do away with a regime hostile to Israel; to begin a process of limited "democratization" in the countries of the Middle East. These reasons overlap, intersect; different officials laid greater emphasis on one or the other. Added to them, the humbling attacks of September 11 served as a kind of catalyst, taking what had been an idea and making it into a seeming necessity. The attacks, after all, had created "a window" during which the frightened and angry American public could be persuaded to support a "war of choice." And such a war, in the eyes of many Bush officials, would not only reaffirm the scope and extent of American power, it would eliminate a threat that had now become intolerable.

"The truth is," notes a British Foreign Office official in one of the documents collected below, "what has changed is not the pace of Saddam Hussein's WMD programs but our tolerance of them post–September 11." Foreign Secretary Straw agrees: "If September 11 had not happened," he writes to Prime Minister Blair,

> it is doubtful that the US would now be considering military action against Iraq. In addition, there has been no credible evidence to link Iraq with [Osama bin Laden] and Al Qaida. Objectively, the threat from Iraq has not worsened as a result of 11 September. What has forever changed is the tolerance of the international community (especially that of the US), the world

having witnessed on September 11 just what determined evil people can these days perpetrate.

Amid all the other reasons, then, it was the September 11
attacks that made war possible—that made it indeed (to use Sir
Richard Dearlove's word) inevitable. The question then
became: How best to convince Americans—the various
bureaucratic factions within the government and the broader
American public—that a war of choice against Iraq must be
fought? And—a lesser but important question—how best to
convince the government and the public of Great Britain, the
critical ally? Saddam's supposed collaboration with al-Qaeda,
though an article of faith among many Bush officials in the
Defense Department, was rejected by powerful figures within
the US and British governments, including the heads of the main
intelligence organizations. "Humanitarian action" to remove
Saddam and replace him with a democratic government, though
supported by some officials, including Deputy Secretary of
Defense Paul Wolfowitz, was not a sufficient "reason to put
American kids' lives at risk," as Wolfowitz admitted after the war.
Saddam's supposed weapons of mass destruction, on the other
hand, had not only been condemned by Security Council
resolution (and thus stood the best chance of any casus belli to

bring the United Nations along) but could be exploited to produce a particularly lurid and thus marketable image of the threat Saddam supposedly posed—an image that suggested an apocalypse comparable to September 11 that George W. Bush *could* act to prevent. To Bush officials, for these reasons and others "having a lot to do with the US government bureaucracy" (in Wolfowitz's words), the weapons seemed best suited to take their place as the public reason for launching a war against Iraq.

Of course, had Saddam's weapons of mass destruction really constituted the sole or even the most important threat he posed, the "UN route" promoted by the British offered a means to remove it. Given time the inspectors could have visited all the "suspect sites" and shown, perhaps by the summer of 2003, what we now know to be the truth: there were no weapons. It is doubtful, though, that the inspectors alone could ever have demonstrated this to the satisfaction of Bush administration officials, for these officials saw in the inspections and the entire "UN route" not a way to disarm Saddam but a way to make possible a war to remove him. The great value of the Downing Street memo is that it makes this distinction unmistakably clear.

In that war "the two key issues," as Prime Minister Blair told his cabinet members on July 23, nearly eight months before it began, would be "whether the military plan worked and whether we had the political strategy to give the military plan the space to work." In the end, neither worked. By following a political strategy that relied on promoting the threat of Saddam's weapons of mass destruction, Bush officials were able to muster sufficient public support in the US to launch the invasion; but they failed to convince the nations of the world, who wanted to let the inspectors continue their work in Iraq, to approve the war. This failure might not have been so damaging, had the military plan put forward by Donald Rumsfeld led American troops and their loyal British allies to the quick and decisive victory that had been promised instead of into a grinding and seemingly endless guerrilla war.

The decision to focus on the weapons, and the failure to find them, has meant that for most Americans—three years and 2,200 American deaths later—the Iraq war's beginning is now as cloudy and indeterminate as its ending. We live with the legacy of exaggerations and lies of the secret way to war: in the distortion of the public debate, the corruption of our politics, and the collapse of the one element essential to fighting a long and inconclusive conflict—the trust and support of the people.

—**MDD**

January 20, 2006

APPENDICES:
THE DOWNING STREET
DOCUMENTS

INTRODUCTION

ON JULY 23, 2002, the senior members of Prime Minister Tony Blair's government met at 10 Downing Street to discuss Iraq. Strictly speaking, "Downing Street memo" refers to the minutes of that meeting, which Matthew Rycroft (an aide to David Manning, Blair's foreign policy adviser) compiled in a two-and-a-half-page memorandum, marked "secret and strictly personal," and distributed to the participants. On May 1, 2005, British journalist Michael Smith made public the document in an article in the London *Sunday Times*.

We reproduce the full text of the Downing Street memo below and follow it with the texts of seven related memoranda, all made public by Smith. Six of these are memos prepared in March 2002 in anticipation of Prime Minister Blair's visit the following month to President Bush's ranch in Crawford, Texas, at which Bush and Blair would discuss Iraq and the prime minister would reaffirm his support for military action to remove Saddam Hussein from power. The documents not only let one trace the evolving strategies within the British government to persuade the Americans to construct a "political context" that would make war more palatable to the British Labour Party and to the international community; they also offer, in their accounts of meetings and meals with American counterparts, glimpses of evolving attitudes within the Bush administration itself. "Condi's enthusiasm for regime change is undimmed," British Foreign Policy Adviser Manning advises Blair, after lunching with the national security adviser in early March—though there "were signs, since we last spoke, of greater awareness of the practical difficulties and political risks." In the evolving "struggle within the Administration between the pro- and con-INC lobbies," Paul Wolfowitz shows himself to be "far more pro-INC than not," reports the British ambassador, after having hosted a Sunday lunch for the deputy secretary of defense. Ahmed Chalabi, the leader of the Iraq exile group, had "a good record in bringing high-grade defectors out of Iraq," said Wolfowitz, though "the CIA stubbornly refused to recognize this."

The March memoranda include:

- "Iraq: Options Paper" (March 8, 2002), which outlines military options for removing Saddam;
- "Iraq: Legal Background" (March 8, 2002), which advises Blair on the legality of using force against Saddam;
- "Your Trip to the US" (March 14, 2002), a memorandum in which the foreign policy adviser tells the prime minister of his talks with Condoleezza Rice;

- "From the Ambassador" (March 18, 2002), in which the British envoy in Washington describes his lunch with then Deputy Secretary of Defense Wolfowitz;
- "Iraq: Advice for the Prime Minister" (March 22, 2002), in which Peter Ricketts, political director of the UK Foreign and Commonwealth and Foreign Office, sets out the political context for military action against Iraq;
- "Crawford/Iraq" (March 25, 2002), in which the British foreign secretary describes how to promote war with Iraq in terms convincing to British Labour Party members and to the international community.

Finally, we include "Iraq: Conditions for Military Action" (July 21, 2002), in which the Cabinet Office sets out "the political conditions" needed to make possible an attack on Iraq. The emphasis, as in the Cabinet meeting two days hence, is on the need to create "an ultimatum...cast in terms Saddam would reject ...but which would not be regarded as unreasonable by the international community." The author concludes that without such an artfully constructed ultimatum, or an Iraqi attack, "we would be most unlikely to achieve a legal base for military action by January 2003"—which is the target date for the war to begin.

I have provided brief introductory notes to each of the documents, which have been lightly edited to remove typographical errors and to explain abbreviations and terms that might be unfamiliar to readers.

—MDD

1

THE DOWNING STREET MEMO

On July 23, 2002, Prime Minister Tony Blair gathered the senior officials of his government together at 10 Downing Street to discuss policy toward Iraq. Those present included Jack Straw, the foreign secretary; Geoffrey Hoon, defence secretary; Lord Goldsmith, attorney general; John Scarlett, head of the Joint Intelligence Committee (or JIC); Sir Richard Dearlove, known as "C," head of MI6 (roughly equivalent to the American CIA); Sir David Manning, foreign policy adviser (equivalent to the national security adviser); Admiral Sir Michael Boyce, chief of the Defence Staff (or CDS); Jonathan Powell, Blair's chief of staff; Alastair Campbell, director of communications and strategy (Blair's political adviser); and Sally Morgan, director of government relations. These officials take up themes that, as a reading of the following memoranda makes clear, have been under discussion within the British government for at least four months. The minutes were taken, and the memorandum drafted, by Matthew Rycroft, a foreign policy aide to Manning.

SECRET AND STRICTLY PERSONAL—UK EYES ONLY

DAVID MANNING
From: Matthew Rycroft
Date: 23 July 2002
S 195 /02

cc: Defence Secretary, Foreign Secretary, Attorney-General, Sir Richard Wilson, John Scarlett, Francis Richards, CDS, C, Jonathan Powell, Sally Morgan, Alastair Campbell

IRAQ: PRIME MINISTER'S MEETING, 23 JULY

Copy addressees and you met the Prime Minister on 23 July to discuss Iraq.

<u>This record is extremely sensitive. No further copies should be made. It should be shown only to those with a genuine need to know its contents.</u>

<u>John Scarlett</u> summarised the intelligence and latest JIC assessment. Saddam's regime was tough and based on extreme fear. The only way to overthrow it was likely to be by massive military action. Saddam was worried and expected an attack, probably by air and land, but he was not convinced that it would be immediate or overwhelming. His regime expected their neighbours to line up with the US. Saddam knew that regular army morale was poor. Real support for Saddam among the public was probably narrowly based.

<u>C</u> reported on his recent talks in Washington. There was a perceptible shift in attitude. Military action was now seen as

inevitable. Bush wanted to remove Saddam, through military action, justified by the conjunction of terrorism and WMD [weapons of mass destruction]. But the intelligence and facts were being fixed around the policy. The NSC had no patience with the UN route, and no enthusiasm for publishing material on the Iraqi regime's record. There was little discussion in Washington of the aftermath after military action.

CDS said that military planners would brief CENTCOM on 1–2 August, Rumsfeld on 3 August and Bush on 4 August. The two broad US options were:

(a) Generated Start. A slow build-up of 250,000 US troops, a short (72 hour) air campaign, then a move up to Baghdad from the south. Lead time of 90 days (30 days preparation plus 60 days deployment to Kuwait).
(b) Running Start. Use forces already in theatre (3 x 6,000), continuous air campaign, initiated by an Iraqi casus belli. Total lead time of 60 days with the air campaign beginning even earlier. A hazardous option.

The US saw the UK (and Kuwait) as essential, with basing in Diego Garcia and Cyprus critical for either option. Turkey and other Gulf states were also important, but less vital. The three main options for UK involvement were:

(i) Basing in Diego Garcia and Cyprus, plus three SF squadrons.
(ii) As above, with maritime and air assets in addition.
(iii) As above, plus a land contribution of up to 40,000, perhaps with a discrete role in Northern Iraq entering from Turkey, tying down two Iraqi divisions.

The <u>Defence Secretary</u> said that the US had already begun "spikes of activity" to put pressure on the regime. No decisions had been taken, but he thought the most likely timing in US minds for military action to begin was January, with the timeline beginning 30 days before the US Congressional elections.

The <u>Foreign Secretary</u> said he would discuss this with Colin Powell this week. It seemed clear that Bush had made up his mind to take military action, even if the timing was not yet decided. But the case was thin. Saddam was not threatening his neighbours, and his WMD capability was less than that of Libya, North Korea or Iran. We should work up a plan for an ultimatum to Saddam to allow back in the UN weapons inspectors. This would also help with the legal justification for the use of force.

The <u>Attorney-General</u> said that the desire for regime change was not a legal base for military action. There were three possible legal bases: self-defence, humanitarian intervention, or UNSC [United Nations Security Council] authorisation. The first and second could not be the base in this case. Relying on UNSCR 1205 of three years ago would be difficult. The situation might of course change.

The <u>Prime Minister</u> said that it would make a big difference politically and legally if Saddam refused to allow in the UN inspectors. Regime change and WMD were linked in the sense that it was the regime that was producing the WMD. There were different strategies for dealing with Libya and Iran. If the political context were right, people would support regime change. The two key issues were whether the military plan worked and whether we had the political strategy to give the military plan the space to work.

On the first, <u>CDS</u> said that we did not know yet if the US battle-plan was workable. The military were continuing to ask lots of questions. For instance, what were the consequences, if Saddam used WMD on day one, or if Baghdad did not collapse and urban warfighting began? <u>You</u> [i.e., David Manning] said that Saddam could also use his WMD on Kuwait. Or on Israel, added the <u>Defence Secretary</u>.

The <u>Foreign Secretary</u> thought the US would not go ahead with a military plan unless convinced that it was a winning strategy. On this, US and UK interests converged. But on the political strategy, there could be US/UK differences. Despite US resistance, we should explore discreetly the ultimatum. Saddam would continue to play hard-ball with the UN. <u>John Scarlett</u> assessed that Saddam would allow the inspectors back in only when he thought the threat of military action was real.

The <u>Defence Secretary</u> said that if the Prime Minister wanted UK military involvement, he would need to decide this early. He cautioned that many in the US did not think it worth going down the ultimatum route. It would be important for the Prime Minister to set out the political context to Bush.

<u>Conclusions:</u>

(a) We should work on the assumption that the UK would take part in any military action. But we needed a fuller picture of US planning before we could take any firm decisions. CDS should tell the US military that we were considering a range of options.

(b) The Prime Minister would revert on the question of whether funds could be spent in preparation for this operation.

(c) CDS would send the Prime Minister full details of the proposed military campaign and possible UK contributions by the end of the week.

(d) The Foreign Secretary would send the Prime Minister the background on the UN inspectors, and discreetly work up the ultimatum to Saddam. He would also send the Prime Minister advice on the positions of countries in the region especially Turkey, and of the key EU [European Union] member states.

(e) John Scarlett would send the Prime Minister a full intelligence update.

(f) We must not ignore the legal issues: the Attorney-General would consider legal advice with FCO/MOD legal advisers.

(I have written separately to commission this follow-up work.)

—MATTHEW RYCROFT

IRAQ: OPTIONS PAPER

This document, drafted by officials in the UK Overseas and Defence Secretariat Cabinet Office and distributed on March 8, 2002, outlines current British policy toward Iraq. The author sets out broad objectives in Iraq, describes the current policy of containment, and evaluates possible changes, including "toughening" containment or moving toward regime change. In discussing the latter the author describes and compares three possible paths toward overthrowing Saddam: providing covert support to opposition groups within Iraq; launching a campaign of aerial bombardment, together with overt support to opposition groups; and initiating a "ground campaign" to invade and occupy Iraq. The paper was among those drafted to prepare Prime Minister Blair for his April 2002 visit to President Bush's ranch in Crawford, Texas.

SECRET UK EYES ONLY

IRAQ: OPTIONS PAPER

SUMMARY

Since 1991, our objective has been to re-integrate a law-abiding Iraq, which does not possess WMD or threaten its neighbors, into the international community. Implicitly, this cannot occur with Saddam Hussein in power. As a least worst option, we have supported a policy of containment which has been partially successful. However:

• Despite sanctions, Iraq continues to develop WMD, although our intelligence is poor. Saddam has used WMD in the past and could do so again if his regime were threatened, though there is no greater threat now than in recent years that Saddam will use WMD; and
• Saddam's brutal regime remains in power and destabilises the Arab and wider Islamic world.

We have two options. We could toughen the existing containment policy. This would increase the pressure on Saddam. It would not re-integrate Iraq into the international community.

The US administration has lost faith in containment and is now considering regime change. The end states could either be a Sunni strongman or a representative government.

The three options for achieving regime change are:

- covert support to opposition groups to mount an uprising/coup;
- air support for opposition groups to mount an uprising/coup; and
- a full-scale ground campaign.

These are not mutually exclusive. Options 1 and/or 2 would be natural precursors to Option 3. The greater the investment of Western forces, the greater our control over Iraq's future, but the greater the cost and the longer we would need to stay. The only certain means to remove Saddam and his elite is to invade and impose a new government. But this could involve nation building over many years. Even a representative government could seek to acquire WMD and build up its conventional forces, so long as Iran and Israel retain their WMD and conventional armouries and there was no acceptable solution to Palestinian grievances.

A legal justification for invasion would be needed. Subject to Law Officers' advice, none currently exists. This makes moving quickly to invade legally very difficult. We should therefore consider a staged approach, establishing international support, building up pressure on Saddam and developing military plans.

There is a lead time of about 6 months to a ground offensive.

CURRENT OBJECTIVES OF UK POLICY

1. Within our objectives of preserving peace and stability in the Gulf and ensuring energy security, our current objectives towards Iraq are:
• the re-integration of a law-abiding Iraq, which does not possess WMD or threaten its neighbours, into the international community. Implicitly this cannot occur with Saddam in power; and
• hence, as the least worst option, we have supported containment of Iraq, by constraining Saddam's ability to re-arm or build up WMD and to threaten his neighbours.

2. Subsidiary objectives are:
• Preserving the territorial integrity of Iraq;
• improving the humanitarian situation of the Iraqi people;
• protecting the Kurds in Northern Iraq;
• sustaining UK/UK co-operation, including, if necessary by moderating US policy; and
• maintaining the credibility and authority of the Security Council.

HAS CONTAINMENT WORKED?

3. Since 1991, the policy of containment has been partially successful;
• Sanctions have effectively frozen Iraq's nuclear programme;
• Iraq has been prevented from rebuilding its conventional arsenal to pre–Gulf War levels;
• ballistic missile programmes have been severely restricted;
• Biological Weapons (BW) and Chemical Weapons (CW) programmes have been hindered;
• No Fly Zones [NFZs] established over northern and southern Iraq have given some protection to the Kurds and the Shia. Although subject to continuing political pressure, the Kurds remain autonomous; and
• Saddam has not succeeded in seriously threatening his neighbours.

4. However:
• Iraq continues to develop weapons of mass destruction, although our intelligence is poor. Iraq has up to 20 650km-range missiles left over from the Gulf War. These are capable of hitting Israel and the Gulf states. Design work for other ballistic missiles over the UN limit of 150km continues. Iraq

continues with the BW and CW programmes and, if it has not already done so, could produce significant quantities of BW agents within days and CW agent within weeks of a decision to do so. We believe it could deliver CBW by a variety of means, including in ballistic missile warheads. There are also some indications of a continuing nuclear programme. Saddam has used WMD in the past and could do so again if his regime were threatened.

• Saddam leads a brutal regime, which impoverishes his people. While in power Saddam is a rallying point for anti-Western sentiment in the Arab and wider Islamic world, and as such a cause of instability; and

• despite UN controls over Iraq's oil revenue under Oil for Food, there is considerable oil and other smuggling.

5. In this context, and against the background of our desire to re-integrate a law-abiding Iraq into the international community, we examine the two following policy options:

• a toughening of the existing containment policy, facilitated by 11 September; and

• regime change by military means: a new departure which would require the construction of a coalition and a legal justification.

TOUGHENING CONTAINMENT

6. This would consist of the following elements:

• full implementation of all relevant UNSCRs [United Nations Security Council resolutions], particularly 687 (1991) and 1284 (1999). We should ensure that the Good Review List (GRL) is introduced in May and that Russia holds to its promise not to block. The signs are positive but continuing pressure is needed. (The GRL focuses sanctions exclusively on preventing shipments of WMD-related and other arms, while allowing other business without scrutiny. As such, it will greatly facilitate legitimate Iraqi commerce under Oil for Food.);

• encourage the US not to block discussions to clarify the modalities of Resolution 1284 once Russian agreement to the GRL has been secured. We should take a hard line on each area for clarification—the purpose of clarification is not to lower the bar on Iraqi compliance; but

• P5 [Permanent Five Member] and Security Council unity would facilitate a specific demand that Iraq re-admit the UN inspectors. Our aim would be to tell Saddam to admit inspectors or face the risk of military action.

• push for tougher action (especially by the US) against states breaking sanctions. This should not discriminate between allies

(Turkey), friends (UAE) and others (especially Syria). It would put real pressure on Saddam either to submit to meaningful inspections or to lash out;

• maintain our present military posture, including in the NFZs, and be prepared to respond robustly to any Iraqi adventurism; and

• continue to make clear (without overtly espousing regime change) our view that Iraq would be better off without Saddam. We could trail the rosy future for Iraq without him in a "Contract with the Iraqi People," although to be at all credible, this would need some detailed work.

7. What could it achieve:

• There will be greater pressure on Saddam. The GRL will make sanctions more attractive to at least some of their detractors. Improving implementation of sanctions would reduce the regime's illicit revenues; and

• the return of UN weapons inspectors would allow greater scrutiny of Iraqi programmes and of Iraqi forces in general. If they found significant evidence of WMD, were expelled or, in face of an ultimatum, not re-admitted in the first place, then this could provide legal justification for large-scale military action (see below).

8. But:

• Some of the difficulties with the existing policy still apply;

• those states in breach of sanctions will want compensation if they are to change tack;

• Saddam is only likely to permit the return of inspectors if he believes the threat of large-scale US military action is imminent and that such concessions would prevent the US from acting decisively. Playing for time, he would then embark on a renewed policy of non co-operation; and

• although containment has held for the past decade, Iraq has progressively increased its international engagement. Even if the GRL makes sanctions more sustainable the sanctions regime could collapse in the long term.

9. Tougher containment would not re-integrate Iraq into the international community as it offers little prospect of removing Saddam. He will continue with his WMD programmes, de-stabilising the Arab and Islamic world, and impoverishing his people. But there is no greater threat now that he will use WMD than there has been in recent years, so continuing containment is an option.

US VIEWS

10. The US has lost confidence in containment. Some in government want Saddam removed. The success of Operation Enduring Freedom, distrust of UN sanctions and inspection regimes, and unfinished business from 1991 are all factors. Washington believes the legal basis for an attack on Iraq already exists. Nor will it necessarily be governed by wider political factors. The US may be willing to work with a much smaller coalition than we think desirable.

REGIME CHANGE

11. In considering the options for regime change below, we need to first consider what sort of Iraq we want. There are two possibilities:

• A Sunni military strongman. He would be likely to maintain Iraqi territorial integrity. Assistance with reconstruction and political rehabilitation could be traded for assurances on abandoning WMD programmes and respecting human rights, particularly of ethnic minorities. The US and other militaries could withdraw quickly. However, there would then be a strong risk of the Iraqi system reverting to type. Military coup could succeed coup until an autocratic, Sunni dictator emerged who

protected Sunni interests. With time he could acquire WMD; or
• a representative broadly democratic government. This would
be Sunni-led but within a federal structure, the Kurds would be
guaranteed autonomy and the Shia fair access to government.
Such a regime would be less likely to develop WMD and threat-
en its neighbours. However, to survive it would require the US
and others to commit to nation building for many years. This
would entail a substantial international security force and help
with reconstruction.

OTHER FACTORS TO CONSIDER: INTERNAL

12. Saddam has a strong grip on power maintained through fear
and patronage. The security and intelligence apparatus, including the Republican and Special Republican Guard, who protect
the regime so effectively, are predominantly drawn from the
Arab Sunni minority (20–25 per cent of the population); many
from Tikrit like Saddam. They fear non-Sunni rule, which
would bring retribution and the end of their privileges. The
regime's success in defeating the 1991 uprising stemmed from
senior Sunni officers looking into the abyss of Shia rule and
preserving their interests by backing Saddam. In the current
circumstances, a military revolt or coup is a remote possibility.

13. Unaided, the Iraqi opposition is incapable of overthrowing the regime. The external opposition is weak, divided and lacks domestic credibility. The predominant group is the Iraqi National Congress (INC), an umbrella organisation led by Ahmad Chalabi, a Shia and convicted fraudster, popular on Capitol Hill. The other major group, the Iraqi National Accord (INA), espouses moderate Arab socialism and is led by another Shia, Ayad Allawi. Neither group has a military capability and both are badly penetrated by Iraqi intelligence. In 1996, a CIA attempt to stir opposition groups ended in wholesale executions. Most Iraqis see the INC/INA as Western stooges.

14. The internal opposition is small and fractured on ethnic and sectarian grounds. There is no effective Sunni Arab opposition. There are 3-4m Kurds in northern Iraq. Most live in the Kurdish Autonomous Zone, established in 1991. The Kurds deploy at least 40,000 lightly armed militia but are divided between two main parties, the Patriotic Union of Kurdistan (PUK) and the Kurdistan Democratic Party (KDP). These groups have an interest in preserving the status quo and are more interested in seeking advantage over the other than allying against Saddam. Divide and rule is easy; in 1996 the KDP assisted the Iraqi Army's expulsion of the PUK and Iraqi opposition groups from Irbil.

15. The Kurds do not co-operate with the Shia Arabs who form 60 per cent of the population. The main Shia opposition group is the Supreme Council for the Islamic Revolution in Iraq (SCIRI), with 3,000–5,000 fighters, but it is tainted by Iranian support. Most Shia would like to have a greater say in Iraqi government, but not necessarily control: they do not want secession, Islamic autonomy or Iranian influence.

REGIONAL

16. Iraq's neighbours have a direct interest in the country's affairs. Iran and Turkey, in particular, are wary of US influence and oppose some opposition groups. Turkey, conscious of its own restive Kurdish minority, will do anything to prevent the establishment of a independent Kurdish state in northern Iraq, including intervention. Iran, also with a Kurdish minority, would also oppose a Kurdish state and is keen to protect the rights of its co-religionists in the south (see FCO [Foreign Office] paper on P5, European and regional view of possible military action against Iraq, attached).

17. We have looked at three options for achieving regime change (we dismissed assassination of Saddam Hussein as an option because it would be illegal):

OPTION 1: COVERT SUPPORT TO OPPOSITION GROUPS

18. The aim would be to bring down the regime by internal revolt, aided by the defection or at least acquiescence of large sections of the Army. A group of Sunni generals, probably from within the Republican Guard, might depose Saddam if they decided the alternative was defeat. This option could be pursued by providing covert intelligence, large-scale financial and Special Forces support to opposition groups. The Kurds would be persuaded to unite and attack into northern Iraq, tying down some Iraqi forces. Simultaneously, in a greater threat to the regime, the Shia would rise up in the southern cities, and in Baghdad.

19. This option also has a very low prospect of success on its own. The external opposition is not strong enough to overthrow Saddam and would be rejected by most Iraqis as a replacement government. The Kurds could only mount a very limited offensive in the north. Mass uprisings in the south would be unlikely. The US failure to support the 1991 uprising remains vivid. The Republican Guard would move against any opposition and any wavering regular Army units. There would also be a high risk of US/coalition forces being captured. The

remaining elements of opposition could be eliminated, buttressing Saddam and his reputation as Arab folk hero. On the other hand, this option has never been pursued in a concerted, single-minded way before and should not be dismissed, at least as a possible precursor to Options 2 and 3.

OPTION 2: AN AIR CAMPAIGN PROVIDING OVERT SUPPORT TO OPPOSITION GROUPS LEADING TO A COUP OR UPRISING

20. The aim would be to assist an internal revolt by providing strategic and tactical air support for opposition groups to move against the regime. Such support would disable Saddam's military and security apparatus. Suspected WMD facilities would also be targeted. Substantial numbers of aircraft and munitions would need to be built up in theatre over a period of months. Any campaign would take several weeks at least, probably several months. Pressure on the regime could be increased by massing ground and naval forces and threatening a land invasion.

21. This option has no guarantee of success. The build-up of pressure might persuade other Sunnis to overthrow Saddam and his family, but there is no guarantee that another Sunni autocrat would be better. Comparisons with Afghanistan are

misleading. Saddam's military and security apparatus is considerable more potent and cohesive. We are not aware of any Karzai figure able to command respect inside and outside Iraq. Arab states would only back the plan if they were sure Saddam would be deposed. At least the co-operation of Kuwait would be needed for the necessary military build-up. The Arab street would oppose an air attack against Iraq, but visibility of a popular uprising could calm Arab public opinion.

OPTION 3: A GROUND CAMPAIGN

22. The aim would be to launch a full-scale ground offensive to destroy Saddam's military machine and remove him from power. A pro-Western regime would be installed which would destroy Iraq's WMD capability, make peace with Iraq's neighbours and give rights to all Iraqis, including ethnic minorities. As in the Gulf War, this would need to be preceded by a major air-offensive to soften up defences.

23. US contingency planning prior to 11 September indicated that such a ground campaign would require 200,000–400,000 troops. The numbers would be roughly half those of 1991 because Iraqi forces are now considerably weaker. Any invasion

force would need to pose a credible threat to Baghdad in order to persuade members of the Sunni military elite that their survival was better served by deserting to the coalition than staying loyal to Saddam. Sufficient air assets would need three months and ground forces at least four–five months to assemble so on logistical grounds a ground campaign is not feasible until autumn 2002. The optimal times to start action are early spring.

24. From a purely military perspective it would be very difficult to launch an invasion from Kuwait alone. Carrier-based aircraft would not be enough because of the need for land-based air-to-air refuelling. To be confident of success, bases either in Jordan or in Saudi Arabia would be required. However, a wider and durable international coalition would be advantageous for both military and political reasons. Securing moderate Arab support would be greatly assisted by the promise of a quick and decisive campaign, and credible action by the US to address the MEPP [Middle East Peace Process].

25. The risks include US and others military casualties. Any coalition would need much tending over the difficult months of preparation for an actual invasion. Iran, fearing further US

encirclement and that it will be invaded next, will be prickly but is likely to remain neutral. With his regime in danger, Saddam could use WMD, either before or during an invasion. Saddam could also target Israel as he did during the Gulf War. Restraining Israel will be difficult. It would try to pre-empt a WMD attack and has certainly made clear that it would retaliate. Direct Israeli military involvement in Iraq would greatly complicate coalition management and risk spreading conflict more widely.

26. None of the above options is mutually exclusive. Options 1 and/or 2 would be natural precursors to Option 3. All options have lead times. If an invasion is contemplated this autumn, then a decision will need to be taken in principle six months in advance. The greater the investment of Western forces, the greater our control over Iraq's future, but the greater the cost and the longer we would need to stay. Option 3 comes closest to guaranteeing regime change. At this stage we need to wait to see which option or combination of options may be favoured by the US government.

27. But it should be noted that even a representative government could seek to acquire WMD and build up its conventional

forces, so long as Iran and Israel retain their WMD and conventional armouries.

LEGAL CONSIDERATIONS

28. A full opinion should be sought from the Law Officers if the above options are developed further. But in summary: CONTAINMENT generally involves the implementation of existing UNSCRs and has a firm legal foundation. Of itself, REGIME CHANGE has no basis in international law. A separate note by FCO Legal Advisors setting out the general legal background and the obligations in the relevant UN Resolutions is attached.

29. In the judgement of the JIC there is no recent evidence of Iraq complicity with international terrorism. There is therefore no justification for action against Iraq based on action in self-defence (Article 51) to combat imminent threats of terrorism as in Afghanistan. However, Article 51 would come into play if Iraq were about to attack a neighbour.

30. Currently, offensive military action against Iraq can only be justified if Iraq is held to be in breach of the Gulf War cease-

fire resolution, 687. 687 imposed obligations on Iraq with regard to the elimination of WMD and monitoring these obligations. But 687 never terminated the authority to use force mandated in UNSCR 678 (1990). Thus a violation of 687 can revive the authorisation to use force in 678.

31. As the cease-fire was proclaimed by the Security Council in 687, it is for the Council to decide whether a breach of obligations has occurred. There is a precedent. UNSCR 1205 (1998), passed after the expulsion of the UN inspectors, stated that in doing so Iraq had acted in flagrant violation of its obligations under 687. In our view, this revived the authority for the use of force under 678 and underpinned Operation Desert Fox. In contrast to general legal opinion, the US assets the right of individual Member States to determine whether Iraq has breached 687, regardless of whether the Council has reached this assessment.

32. For the P5 and the majority of the Council to take the view that Iraq was in breach of 687:
• they would need to be convinced that Iraq was in breach of its obligations regarding WMD and ballistic missiles. Such proof would need to be incontrovertible and of large-scale activity.

Current intelligence is insufficiently robust to meet this criterion. Even with overriding proof China, France and Russia, in particular, would need considerable lobbying to approve or acquiesce in a new resolution authorising military action against Iraq. Concessions in other policy areas might be needed. However, many Western states, at least, would not wish to oppose the US on such a major issue; or
• if P5 unity could be obtained, Iraq refused to readmit UN inspectors after a clear ultimatum by the UN Security Council; or
• the UN inspectors were re-admitted to Iraq and found sufficient evidence of WMD activity or were again expelled trying to do so.

CONCLUSION

33. In sum, despite the considerable difficulties, the use of overriding force in a ground campaign is the only option that we can be confident will remove Saddam and bring Iraq back into the international community.

34. To launch such a campaign would require a staged approach:

- winding up the pressure: increasing the pressure on Saddam through tougher containment. Stricter implementation of sanctions and a military build-up will frighten his regime. A refusal to admit UN inspectors, or their admission and subsequent likely frustration, which resulted in an appropriate finding by the Security Council, could provide the justification for military action. Saddam would try to prevent this, although he has miscalculated before;
- careful planning: detailed military planning on the various invasion and basing options, and when appropriate force deployment;
- coalition building: diplomatic work to establish an international coalition to provide the broadest political and military support to a ground campaign. This will need to focus on China, France and particularly Russia who have the ability to block action in the UN Security Council and on the other Europeans. Special attention will need to be paid to moderate Arab states and to Iran;
- incentives: as an incentive guarantees will need to be made with regard to Iraqi territorial integrity. Plans should be worked up in advance of the great benefits the international community could provide for a post-Saddam Iraq and its people. These should be published;

• tackling other regional issues: an effort to engage the US in a serious effort to re-energise the MEPP [Middle East Peace Plan] would greatly assist coalition building; and
• sensitising the public: a media campaign to warn of the dangers that Saddam poses and to prepare public opinion both in the UK and abroad.

35. The US should be encouraged to consult widely on its plans.

OVERSEAS AND DEFENCE SECRETARIAT
CABINET OFFICE
8 MARCH 2002

2

IRAQ: LEGAL BACKGROUND

This document, dated March 8, 2002, was drafted by officials in the UK Foreign Office to suggest how an attack on Iraq might be legally justified. Great Britain and its allies might contend that they are defending themselves from attack, moving to "prevent an overwhelming humanitarian catastrophe," or acting to enforce UN Security Council resolutions. To argue self-defense, the author concludes, "there must be more than 'a threat'" of attack by Iraq; rather "an armed attack [must be] actual or imminent." To argue humanitarian intervention, "the catastrophe must be clear and well documented [and] and there must be no other means short of war to prevent it." In the matter of the United Nations, however, the author contends that resolutions passed in 1998, which condemned Iraq's decision to halt cooperation with weapons inspectors, "had the effect of causing the authorisation to use force in resolution 678"—which eleven years before approved "all necessary means" to expel Iraqi armies from Kuwait—"to revive."

CONFIDENTIAL

IRAQ: LEGAL BACKGROUND

(i) Use of Force: (a) Security Council Resolutions
                    (b) Self-defence
                    (c) Humanitarian Intervention

(ii) No Fly Zones

(iii) Security Council Resolutions relevant to the sanctions regime

(iv) Security Council Resolutions relating to UNMOVIC [United Nations Monitoring, Verification and Inspection Commission]

(i) Use of Force: (a) Security Council Resolutions relevant to the Authorisation of the Use of Force

1. Following its invasion and annexation of Kuwait, the Security Council authorised the use of force against Iraq in resolution 675 (1990); this resolution authorised coalition forces to use all necessary means to force Iraq to withdraw, and to restore international peace and security in the area. This resolution gave a legal basis for Operation Desert Storm, which was brought to an end by the cease-fire set out by the Council in resolution 687 (1991). The conditions for the cease-fire in that resolution (and subsequent resolutions) imposed obligations on Iraq with regard to the elimination of WMD and monitoring of its obligations. Resolution 687 (1991) suspended but

did not terminate the authority to use force in resolutions 678 (1990).

2. In the UK's view a violation of Iraq's obligations which undermines the basis of the cease-fire in resolution 687 (1991) can revive the authorisation to use force in resolution 678 (1990). As the cease-fire was proclaimed by the Council in resolution 687 (1991), it is for the Council to assess whether any such breach of those obligations has occurred. The US have a rather different view: they maintain that the assessment of breach is for individual member States. We are not aware of any other State which supports this view.

3. The authorisation to use force contained in resolution 678 (1990) has been revived in this way on certain occasions. For example, when Iraq refused to cooperate with the UN Special Commission (UNSCOM) in 1997/8, a series of SCRs condemned the decision as unacceptable. In resolution 1205 (1998) the Council condemned Iraq's decision to end all cooperation with UNSCOM as a flagrant violation of Iraq's obligations under resolution 687 (1991), and restated that the effective operation of UNSCOM was essential for the implementation of that resolution. In our view these resolutions had the

effect of causing the authorisation to use force in resolutions 678 (1991) to revive, which provided a legal basis for Operation Desert Fox. In a letter to the President of the Security Council in 1998 we stated that the objective of that operation was to seek compliance by Iraq with the obligations laid down by the Council, that the operation was undertaken only when it became apparent that there was no other way of achieving compliance by Iraq, and that the action was limited to what was necessary to secure this objective.

4. The more difficult issue is whether we are still able to rely on the same legal base for the use of force more than three years after the adoption of resolution 1205 (1998). Military action in 1998 (and on previous occasions) followed on from specific decisions of the Council; there has now not been any significant decision by the Council since 1998. Our interpretation of resolutions 1205 was controversial anyway; many of our partners did not think the legal basis was sufficient as the authority to use force was not explicit. Reliance on it now would be unlikely to receive any support.

USE OF FORCE: (B) SELF-DEFENCE

5. The conditions that have to be met for the exercise of the right of self-defence are well known:
i) There must be an armed attack upon a State or such an attack must be imminent;
ii) The use of force must be necessary and other means to reverse/avert the attack must be unavailable;
iii) The acts in self-defence must be proportionate and strictly confined to the object of stopping the attack.

The right of self-defence may only be exercised until the Security Council has taken measures necessary to ensure international peace and security and anything done in exercise of the right of self-defence must be immediately reported to the Council.

6. For the exercise of the right of self-defence there must be more than "a threat." There has to be an armed attack, actual or imminent. The development of possession of nuclear weapons does not in itself amount to an armed attack; what would be needed would be clear evidence of an imminent attack. During the Cold War there was certainly a threat in the sense that various States had nuclear weapons which they might, at short notice, unleash upon each other. But that did not mean the mere possession of nuclear weapons, or indeed their possession in

time of high tension or attempt to obtain them, was sufficient to justify pre-emptive action. And when Israel attacked an Iraqi nuclear reactor, near Baghdad, on 7 June 1981 it was "strongly condemned" by the Security Council (acting unanimously) as a "military attack...in clear violation of the Charter of the United Nations and the norms of international conduct."

USE OF FORCE: (C) HUMANITARIAN INTERVENTION

7. In the UK view the use of force may be justified if the action is taken to prevent an overwhelming humanitarian catastrophe. The limits to this highly contentious doctrine are not clearly defined, but we would maintain that the catastrophe must be clear and well documented, that there must be no other means short of the use of force which could prevent it, and that the measures taken must be proportionate. This doctrine partly underlies the very limited action taken by allied aircraft to patrol the No Fly Zones in Iraq (following action by Saddam to repress the Kurds and the Shia in the early 90s), which involved occasional and limited use of force by those aircraft in self-defence. The application of this doctrine depends on the circumstances at any given time, but it is clearly exceptional.

(II) NO FLY ZONES (NFZs)

8. The NFZs over Northern and Southern Iraq are not established by UN Security Council Resolutions. They were established in 1991 and 1992 on the basis that they were necessary and proportionate steps taken to prevent a humanitarian crisis. Prior to the establishment of the Northern NFZ the Security Council had adopted resolution 688 (1991) on 5 April 1991 in which the Council stated that it was gravely concerned by the repression of the Iraqi civilian population in many parts of Iraq, including most recently in Kurdish populated areas, which had led to a massive refugee flow, and that it was deeply disturbed by the magnitude of the human suffering involved. The resolution condemned that repression of the Iraqi civilian population and demanded that Iraq immediately end the repression. In our view the purpose of the NFZs is to monitor Iraqi compliance with the provisions of resolution 688. UK and US aircraft patrolling the NFZs are entitled to use force in self-defence where such a use of force is a necessary and proportionate response to actual or imminent attack from Iraqi ground systems.

9. The US have on occasion claimed that the purpose of the

NFZs is to enforce Iraqi compliance with resolutions 687 or 688. This view is not consistent with resolution 687, which does not deal with the repression of the Iraqi population, or with resolution 688, which was not adopted under Chapter VII of the UN Charter and does not contain any provision for enforcement. Nor (as it is sometimes claimed) were the current NFZs provided for in the Safwan agreement, a provisional agreement between coalition and Iraqi commanders of 3 March 1991, laying down military conditions for the cease-fire which did not contain any reference to the NFZs.

(III) SECURITY COUNCIL RESOLUTIONS RELEVANT TO THE SANCTIONS REGIME

10. The sanctions regime against Iraq was established by resolution 661 (1990) of 8 August 1990, which, following the invasion of Kuwait by Iraq, decides that all states shall prevent the import into their territories of any commodities originating in Iraq, the sale or supply to Iraq of any commodities other than medical supplies, and, in humanitarian circumstances, foodstuffs, and that Iraqi funds and financial resources should be frozen. Resolution 661 remains in force. The major exception to the sanctions regime is the oil for food programme,

which was established by resolution 986 (1995), and permits oil exports (in unlimited amounts following resolution 1284 (1999)) by Iraq on condition that the purchase price is paid into an escrow account established by the UN Secretary-General, and the funds to that account are used to meet the humanitarian needs of the Iraqi people through the export of medicine, health supplies, foodstuffs and materials and supplies for essential civilian needs. The escrow account is also used to fund the UN Compensation Commission and to meet the operating costs of the UN, including those of UNMOVIC (see below).

11. The oil for food programme is renewed by the Security Council at (usually) 6 monthly intervals, most recently by resolution 1382 (211) of 29 November 2001. Under that resolution the Council also decided that it would adopt, by 13 May 2002, procedures which would improve the flow of goods to Iraq, other than arms and other potential dual use goods on a Good Review List. The US are currently reviewing the final details of the list with the Russians.

12. In resolution 687 (1991) the Council decided that the prohibition against the import of goods from Iraq should have

no further force when Iraq has completed all the actions contemplated in paragraphs 8–13 of that resolution concerning Iraq's WMD programme. Iraq has still not complied with this condition. Under paragraph 21 of resolution 687, the Council decided to review the prohibition against the supply of commodities to Iraq every 60 days in the light of the policies and practices of the Iraqi government, including the implementation of all the relevant resolutions of the Council, for the purpose of determining whether to reduce or lift them. These regular reviews are currently suspended as a result of Iraqi noncompliance with the Council's demands.

13. The intention of the Council to act in accordance with resolution 687 on the termination of these prohibitions has been regularly reaffirmed, including in resolution 1284 (1999). Paragraph 33 of that resolution also contains a complex formula for the suspension of economic sanctions against Iraq for renewable periods of 120 days, if UNMOVIC and the IAEA [International Atomic Energy Agency] report cooperation in all respects by Iraq in fulfilling work programmed with those bodies for a period of 120 days after a reinforced system of monitoring and verification in Iraq becomes fully operational. Iraq has never complied with these conditions.

(iv) SECURITY COUNCIL RESOLUTIONS RELATING TO UNMOVIC

14. UNMOVIC was established under resolution 687 (1991) (the cease-fire resolution). UNMOVIC is to undertake the responsibilities of the former Special Commission under resolution 687 relating to the destruction of Iraqi CBW and ballistic missiles with a range of over 150 kilometres and the ongoing monitoring and verification of Iraq's compliance with these obligations. Like the Special Commission, UNMOVIC is to be allowed unconditional access to all Iraqi facilities, equipment and records as well as to Iraqi officials. Under paragraph 7 of resolution 1284 UNMOVIC and the IAEA were given the responsibility of drawing up a work programme which would include the implementation of a reinforced system of ongoing monitoring and verification (OMV) and key remaining disarmament tasks to be completed by Iraq, which constitute the governing standard of Iraqi compliance. There are currently no UNMOVIC personnel in Iraq, and the reinforced OMV system has not been implemented because of Iraq's refusal to cooperate.

"I HAD DINNER WITH CONDI"

In a memorandum dated March 14, 2002, Blair's foreign policy adviser, Sir David Manning, reports to his boss on his discussions with his Washington opposite number, then National Security Adviser Condoleezza Rice. Manning reports that he reassured Rice that Blair "would not budge in your support for regime change" but "it must be carefully done and produce the right result. Failure is not an option." In a passage revealing for what it says about the "special relationship," Manning assures Blair that his "talks with Condi convinced me that Bush wants to hear your views on Iraq before taking decisions. . . . This gives you real influence." Whatever influence Blair might have on the Americans, however, there are plainly limits, as Manning suggests in this dark observation on the war that the allies will launch almost precisely a year later: "I think there is a real risk that the Administration underestimates the difficulties. They may agree that failure isn't an option, but this does not mean that they will avoid it."

SECRET—STRICTLY PERSONAL

FROM: DAVID MANNING
DATE: 14 MARCH 2002

CC: JONATHAN POWELL

PRIME MINISTER

YOUR TRIP TO THE US

I had dinner with Condi on Tuesday; and talks and lunch with her and NSC team on Wednesday (to which Christopher Meyer also came). These were good exchanges, and particularly frank when we were one-on-one at dinner. I attach the records in case you want to glance.

IRAQ

We spent a long time at dinner on IRAQ. It is clear that Bush is grateful for your support and has registered that you are getting flak. I said that you would not budge in your support for regime change but you had to manage a press, a Parliament and a public opinion that was very different than anything in the

States. And you would not budge either in your insistence that, if we pursued regime change, it must be very carefully done and produce the right result. Failure was not an option.

Condi's enthusiasm for regime change is undimmed. But there were some signs, since we last spoke, of greater awareness of the practical difficulties and political risks. (See the attached piece by Seymour Hersh which Christopher Meyer says gives a pretty accurate picture of the uncertain state of the debate in Washington.)

From what she said, Bush has yet to find the answers to the big questions:
• how to persuade international opinion that military action against Iraq is necessary and justified;
• what value to put on the exiled Iraqi opposition;
• how to coordinate a US/allied military campaign with internal opposition (assuming there is any);
• what happens on the morning after?

Bush will want to pick your brains. He will also want to hear whether he can expect coalition support. I told Condi that we realised that the Administration could go it alone if it chose. But if it wanted company, it would have to take account of the concerns of its potential coalition partners. In particular:

• the UN dimension. The issue of the weapons inspectors must be handled in a way that would persuade European and wider opinion that the US was conscious of the international framework, and the insistence of many countries on the need for a legal base. Renewed refusal by Saddam to accept unfettered inspections would be a powerful argument;

• the paramount importance of tackling Israel/Palestine. Unless we did, we could find ourselves bombing Iraq and losing the Gulf.

YOUR VISIT TO THE RANCH

No doubt we need to keep a sense of perspective. But my talks with Condi convinced me that Bush wants to hear your views on Iraq before taking decisions. He also wants your support. He is still smarting from the comments by other European leaders on his Iraq policy.

This gives you real influence: on the public relations strategy; on the UN and weapons inspections; and on US planning for any military campaign. This could be critically important. I think there is a real risk that the Administration underestimates the difficulties. They may agree that failure isn't an option, but this does not mean that they will avoid it.

Will the Sunni majority really respond to an uprising led by Kurds and Shias? Will Americans really put in enough ground troops to do the job if the Kurdish/Shi'ite stratagem fails? Even if they do, will they be willing to take the sort of casualties that the Republican Guard may inflict on them if it turns out to be an urban war, and Iraqi troops don't conveniently collapse in a heap as Richard Perle and others confidently predict? They need to answer these, and other tough questions, in a more convincing way than they have so far before concluding that they can do the business.

The talks at the ranch will also give you the chance to push Bush on the Middle East. The Iraq factor means that there may never be a better opportunity to get this Administration to give sustained attention to reviving the MEPP [Middle East Peace Process].

"WOLFOWITZ CAME TO SUNDAY LUNCH"

On March 18, 2002, Sir Christopher Meyer, the British ambassador in Washington, writes to Sir David Manning describing his Sunday lunch with Deputy Secretary of Defense Paul Wolfowitz. Sir Christopher is notably blunt on the evolving strategy to justify the war: "We backed regime change, but the plan had to be clever. . . . I then went through the need to wrongfoot Saddam on the inspectors and UN [Security Council Resolutions]. . . ." The memo is also interesting for the picture it gives of the political struggle within the administration over the politics of post-Saddam Iraq, notably between supporters and opponents of Iraqi National Congress leader Ahmed Chalabi. To replace Saddam with "something like a functioning democracy," Wolfowitz says, there must be "a coalition of all the parties"—an idea that seems to have been discarded soon after the invasion a year later.

CONFIDENTIAL AND PERSONAL

British Embassy Washington

From the Ambassador
Christopher Meyer KCMG

18 March 2002

Sir David Manning KCMG
No 10 Downing Street

IRAQ AND AFGHANISTAN:
CONVERSATION WITH WOLFOWITZ

1. Paul Wolfowitz, the Deputy Secretary of Defense, came to
Sunday lunch on 17 March.

2. On Iraq I opened by sticking very closely to the script that
you used with Condi Rice last week. We backed regime change,
but the plan had to be clever and failure was not an option. It
would be a tough sell for us domestically, and probably tougher
elsewhere in Europe. The US could go it alone if it wanted to.
But if it wanted to act with partners, there had to be a strategy
for building support for military action against Saddam. I then
went through the need to wrongfoot Saddam on the inspectors
and the UNSCRs and the critical importance of the MEPP as an
integral part of the anti-Saddam strategy. If all this could be
accomplished skillfully, we were fairly confident that a number
of countries would come on board.

3. I said that the UK was giving serious thought to publishing a paper that would make the case against Saddam. If the UK were to join with the US in any operation against Saddam, we would have to be able to take a critical mass of parliamentary and public opinion with us. It was extraordinary how people had forgotten how bad he was.

4. Wolfowitz said that he fully agreed. He took a slightly different position from others in the Administration, who were focussed on Saddam's capacity to develop weapons of mass destruction. The WMD danger was of course crucial to the public case against Saddam, particularly the potential linkage to terrorism. But Wolfowitz thought it indispensable to spell out in detail Saddam's barbarism. This was well documented from what he had done during the occupation of Kuwait, the incursion into Kurdish territory, the assault on the Marsh Arabs, and to his own people. A lot of work had been done on this towards the end of the first Bush administration. Wolfowitz thought that this would go a long way to destroying any notion of moral equivalence between Iraq and Israel. I said that I had been forcefully struck, when addressing university audiences in the US, how ready students were to gloss over Saddam's crimes and to blame the US and the UK for the suffering of the Iraqi people.

5. Wolfowitz said that it was absurd to deny the link between terrorism and Saddam. There might be doubt about the alleged meeting in Prague between Mohammed Atta, the lead hijacker on 9/11, and Iraqi intelligence (did we, he asked, know anything more about this meeting?). But there were other substantiated cases of Saddam giving comfort to terrorists, including someone involved in the first attack on the World Trade Center (the latest New Yorker apparently has a story about links between Saddam and Al Qaeda operating in Kurdistan).

6. I asked for Wolfowitz's take on the struggle inside the Administration between the pro- and anti-INC [Iraqi National Congress] lobbies (well documented in Sy Hersh's recent New Yorker piece, which I gave you). He said that he found himself between the two sides (but as the conversation developed, it became clear that Wolfowitz was far more pro-INC than not). He said that he was strongly opposed to what some were advocating: a coalition including all outside factions except the INC (INA, KDP, PUK, SCRI) . This would not work. Hostility towards the INC was in reality hostility toward Chalabi. It was true that Chalabi was not the easiest person to work with. But he had a good record in bringing high-grade defectors out of Iraq. The CIA stubbornly refused to recognize this. They unreasonably

denigrated the INC because of their fixation with Chalabi. When I mentioned that the INC was penetrated by Iraqi intelligence, Wolfowitz commented that this was probably the case with all the opposition groups: it was something we would have to live with. As to the Kurds, it was true that they were living well (another point to be made in any public dossier on Saddam) and that they feared provoking an incursion by Baghdad. But there were good people among the Kurds, including in particular Salih (?) of the PUK. Wolfowitz brushed over my reference to the absence of Sunni in the INC: there was a big difference between Iraqi and Iranian Shia. The former just wanted to be rid of Saddam.

7. Wolfowitz was pretty dismissive of the desirability of a military coup and of the defector generals in the wings. The latter had blood on their hands. The important thing was to try to have Saddam replaced by something like a functioning democracy. Though imperfect, the Kurdish model was not bad. How to achieve this, I asked? Only through a coalition of all the parties was the answer (we did not get into military planning).

IRAQ: ADVICE FOR THE PRIME MINISTER

On March 22, 2002, Sir Peter Ricketts, political director of the UK Foreign Office, writes to his boss, Jack Straw, to suggest what the foreign secretary should tell Blair as the prime minister prepares to visit Bush in Crawford. Like Manning, Ricketts reassures Blair about his influence: "By sharing Bush's broad objectives, the Prime Minister can bring home to Bush some of the realities which will be less evident from Washington." Among those, a clearer view of the Iraq threat: "The truth is that what has changed is not the pace of Saddam Hussein's WMD programmes, but our tolerance of them post–11 September." Meantime "US scrambling to establish a link between Iraq and Al Qaida is so far frankly unconvincing." Bush must be persuaded to "focus on elimination of WMD, and show that he is serious about UN inspectors. . . ." Such a policy is "win/win for him" since either Saddam "against all odds allows the inspectors to operate freely, in which case we can further hobble his WMD programmes, or he blocks/hinders, and we are on stronger ground for switching to other methods." A third alternative—that Saddam might admit the inspectors who would then find nothing—goes unmentioned.

CONFIDENTIAL AND PERSONAL

PR.121

From: P F Ricketts
Political Director

Date: 22 March 2002

CC: PUS

SECRETARY OF STATE

IRAQ: ADVICE FOR THE PRIME MINISTER

1. You invited thoughts for your personal note to the Prime Minister covering the official advice (we have put up a draft minute separately). Here are mine.

2. By sharing Bush's broad objective, the Prime Minister can help shape how it is defined, and the approach to achieving it. In the process, he can bring home to Bush some of the realities which will be less evident from Washington. He can help Bush make good

decisions by telling him things his own machine probably isn't.

3. But broad support for the objective brings two real problems which need discussing.

4. First, the THREAT. The truth is that what has changed is not the pace of Saddam Hussein's WMD programmes, but our tolerance of them post–11 September. This is not something we need to be defensive about, but attempts to claim otherwise publicly will increase scepticism about our case. I am relieved that you decided to postpone publication of the unclassified document. My meeting yesterday showed that there is more work to do to ensure that the figures are accurate and consistent with those of the US. But even the best survey of Iraq's WMD programmes will not show much advance in recent years on the nuclear, missile or CW/BW fronts: the programmes are extremely worrying but have not, as far as we know, been stepped up.

5. US scrambling to establish a link between Iraq and Al Qaida is so far frankly unconvincing. To get public and Parliamentary support for military operations, we have to be convincing that:
• the threat is so serious/imminent that it is worth sending our troops to die for;

• it is qualitatively different from the threat posed by other proliferators who are closer to achieving nuclear capability (including Iran).

We can make the case on qualitative difference (only Iraq has attacked a neighbour, used CW and fired missiles against Israel). The overall strategy needs to include re-doubled efforts to tackle other proliferators, including Iran, in other ways (the UK/French ideas on greater IAEA activity are helpful here). But we are still left with a problem of bringing public opinion to accept the imminence of a threat from Iraq. This is something the Prime Minister and President need to have a frank discussion about.

6. The second problem is the END STATE. Military operations need clear and compelling military objectives. For Kosovo, it was: Serbs out, Kosovars back, peace-keepers in. For Afghanistan, destroying the Taleban and Al Qaida military capability. For Iraq, "regime change" does not stack up. It sounds like a grudge between Bush and Saddam. Much better, as you have suggested, to make the objective ending the threat to the international community from Iraqi WMD before Saddam uses it or gives it to terrorists. This is at once easier to justify in terms of

international law, but also more demanding. Regime change which produced another Sunni General still in charge of an active Iraqi WMD programme would be a bad outcome (not least because it would be almost impossible to maintain UN sanctions on a new leader who came in promising a fresh start). As with the fight against UBL [Usama bin Laden], Bush would do well to de-personalise the objective" focus on elimination of WMD, and show that he is serious about UN Inspectors as the first choice means of achieving that (it is win/win for him: either Saddam against all the odds allows Inspectors to operate freely, in which case we can further hobble his WMD programmes, or he blocks/hinders, and we are on stronger ground for switching to other methods).

7. Defining the end state in this way, and working through the UN, will of course also help maintain a degree of support among the Europeans, and therefore fits with another major message which the Prime Minister will want to get across: the importance of positioning Iraq as a problem for the international community as a whole, not just for the US.

PETER RICKETTS
CONFIDENTIAL AND PERSONAL

FOREIGN SECRETARY STRAW ON "CRAWFORD/IRAQ"

On March 25, 2002, Jack Straw writes Blair about his upcoming visit to Bush. The foreign secretary's tone is sober: "The rewards from your visit to Crawford will be few. The risks are high, both for you and for the Government." What has changed is not the threat from Iraq but "the tolerance of the international community (especially that of the US), the world having witnessed on September 11 just what determined evil people can these days perpetrate." Straw urges Blair to focus on Iraq's "flagrant breach of international legal obligations" and to take from this "the core of a strategy" which would have at its heart "the unfettered readmission of weapons inspectors." And, like his colleagues, Straw offer premonitions of a darker future: "We have also to answer the big question—what will this action achieve? There seems to be a larger hole in this than on anything." Though assessments from the US "have assumed regime change..., none has satisfactorily answered how that regime change is to be secured, and how there can be any certainty that the replacement regime will be better."

SECRET AND PERSONAL

PM/02/019
PRIME MINISTER

CRAWFORD/IRAQ

1. The rewards from your visit to Crawford will be few. The risks are high, both for you and for the Government. I judge that there is at present no majority inside the PLP [Parliamentary Labour Party] for any military action against Iraq (alongside a greater readiness in the PLP to surface their concerns). Colleagues know that Saddam and the Iraqi regime are bad. Making that case is easy. But we have a long way to go to convince them as to:

(a) the scale of the threat from Iraq and why this has got worse recently;

(b) what distinguishes the Iraqi threat from that of e.g. Iran and North Korea so as to justify military action;

(c) the justification for any military action in terms of international law; and

144

(d) whether the consequence of military action really would be a compliant, law-abiding replacement government.

2. The whole exercise is made much more difficult to handle as long as conflict between Israel and the Palestinians is so acute.

THE SCALE OF THE THREAT

3. The Iraqi regime plainly poses a most serious threat to its neighbours, and therefore to international security. However, in the documents so far presented it has been hard to glean whether the threat from Iraq is so significantly different from that of Iran and North Korea as to justify military action (see below).

WHAT IS WORSE NOW?

4. If 11 September had not happened, it is doubtful that the US would now be considering military action against Iraq. In addition, there has been no credible evidence to link Iraq with UBL and Al Qaida. Objectively, the threat from Iraq has not worsened as a result of 11 September. What has however

changed is the tolerance of the international community (especially that of the US), the world having witnessed on September 11 just what determined evil people can these days perpetrate.

THE DIFFERENCE BETWEEN IRAQ, IRAN AND NORTH KOREA

5. By linking these countries together in this "axis of evil" speech, President Bush implied an identity between them not only in terms of their threat, but also in terms of the action necessary to deal with the threat. A lot of work will now need to be done to delink the three, and to show why military action against Iraq is so much more justified than against Iran and North Korea. The heart of this case—that Iraq poses a unique and present danger—rests on the facts that it:

- invaded a neighbour;
- has used WMD and would use them again;
- is in breach of nine UNSCRs.

THE POSITION IN INTERNATIONAL LAW

6. That Iraq is in flagrant breach of international legal obliga-

tions imposed on it by the UNSC provides us with the core of a strategy, and one which is based on international law. Indeed, if the argument is to be won, the whole case against Iraq and in favour (if necessary) of military action needs to be narrated with reference to the international rule of law

.

7. We also have better to sequence the explanation of what we are doing and why. Specifically, we need to concentrate in the early stages on:

• making operational the sanctions regime foreshadowed by UNSCR 1382;

• demanding the readmission of weapons inspectors, but this time to operate in a free and unfettered way (a similar formula to that which Cheney used at your joint press conference, as I recall).

8. I know there are those who say that an attack on Iraq would be justified whether or not weapons inspectors were readmitted. But I believe that a demand for the unfettered readmission of weapons inspectors is essential, in terms of public explanation, and in terms of legal sanction for any subsequent military action.

9. Legally there are two potential elephant traps:

(i) regime change per se is no justification for military action; it could form part of the method of any strategy, but not a goal. Of course, we may want credibly to assert that regime change is an essential part of the strategy by which we have to achieve our ends—that of the elimination of Iraq's WMD capacity; but the latter has to be the goal;

(ii) on whether any military action would require a fresh UNSC mandate (Desert Fox did not). The US are likely to oppose any idea of a fresh mandate. On the other side, the weight of legal advice here is that a fresh mandate may well be required. There is no doubt that a new UNSCR would transform the climate in the PLP. Whilst that (a new mandate) is very unlikely, given the US's position, a draft resolution against military action with 13 in favour (or handsitting) and two vetoes against could play very badly here.

THE CONSEQUENCES OF ANY MILITARY ACTION

10. A legal justification is a necessary but far from sufficient precondition for military action. We have also to answer the big

question—what will this action achieve? There seems to be a larger hole in this than on anything. Most of the assessments from the US have assumed regime change as a means of eliminating Iraq's WMD threat. But none has satisfactorily answered how that regime change is to be secured, and how there can be any certainty that the replacement regime will be better.

11. Iraq has had NO history of democracy so no one has this habit or experience.

(JACK STRAW)

Foreign and Commonwealth Office
25 March 2002

SECRET AND PERSONAL

IRAQ: CONDITIONS FOR MILITARY ACTION

On July 21, 2005, officials in the Cabinet Office produce a memorandum summarizing the state of play on Iraq. Though Prime Minister Blair's famous visit to Crawford is now three months past, little in the discussion seems to have changed. Ministers are invited once again to observe that in the US government "little thought has been given to creating the political conditions for military action, or the aftermath and how to shape it." The officials renew their strategy of extracting from the Security Council "an ultimatum [on weapons inspectors] in terms which Saddam would reject . . . and which would not be regarded as unreasonable by the international community." Finally, and once again, the author warns that a "post-war occupation of Iraq could lead to a protracted and costly nation-building exercise. As already made clear, the US military plans are virtually silent on this point." The British appeal for "further work . . . to define more precisely the means by which the desired endstate would be created." In Washington, however, that "virtual silence" remains.

[Note: In the version that was leaked to the press, the last page of the document is missing.]

PERSONAL SECRET UK EYES ONLY

IRAQ: CONDITIONS FOR MILITARY ACTION (A Note by Officials)

SUMMARY

Ministers are invited to:

(1) Note the latest position on US military planning and timescales for possible action.

(2) Agree that the objective of any military action should be a stable and law-abiding Iraq, within present borders, co-operating with the international community, no longer posing a threat to its neighbours or international security, and abiding by its international obligations on WMD.

(3) Agree to engage the US on the need to set military plans within a realistic political strategy, which includes identifying the succession to Saddam Hussein and creating the conditions necessary to justify government military action, which might include an ultimatum for the return of UN weapons inspectors to Iraq. This should include a call from the Prime Minister to

President Bush ahead of the briefing of US military plans to the President on 4 August.

(4) Note the potentially long lead times involved in equipping UK Armed Forces to undertake operations in the Iraqi theatre and agree that the MOD [Ministry of Defence] should bring forward proposals for the procurement of Urgent Operational Requirements under cover of the lessons learned from Afghanistan and the outcome of SR2002.

(5) Agree to the establishment of an ad hoc group of officials under Cabinet Office Chairmanship to consider the development of an information campaign to be agreed with the US.

INTRODUCTION

1. The US Government's military planning for action against Iraq is proceeding apace. But, as yet, it lacks a political framework. In particular, little thought has been given to creating the political conditions for military action, or the aftermath and how to shape it.

2. When the Prime Minister discussed Iraq with President Bush at Crawford in April he said that the UK would support military

action to bring about regime change, provided that certain conditions were met: efforts had been made to construct a coalition/shape public opinion, the Israel-Palestine Crisis was quiescent, and the options for action to eliminate Iraq's WMD through the UN weapons inspectors had been exhausted.

3. We need now to reinforce this message and to encourage the US Government to place its military planning within a political framework, partly to forestall the risk that military action is precipitated in an unplanned way by, for example, an incident in the No Fly Zones. This is particularly important for the UK because it is necessary to create the conditions in which we could legally support military action. Otherwise we face the real danger that the US will commit themselves to a course of action which we would find very difficult to support.

4. In order to fulfill the conditions set out by the Prime Minister for UK support for military action against Iraq, certain preparations need to be made, and other considerations taken into account. This note sets them out in a form which can be adapted for use with the US Government. Depending on US intentions, a decision in principle may be needed soon on whether and in what form the UK takes part in military action.

THE GOAL

5. Our objective should be a stable and law-abiding Iraq, within present borders, co-operating with the international community, no longer posing a threat to its neighbours or to international security, and abiding by its international obligations on WMD. It seems unlikely that this could be achieved while the current Iraqi regime remains in power. US military planning unambiguously takes as its objective the removal of Saddam Hussein's regime, followed by elimination of Iraqi WMD. It is however, by no means certain, in the view of UK officials, that one would necessarily follow from the other. Even if regime change is a necessary condition for controlling Iraqi WMD, it is certainly not a sufficient one.

US MILITARY PLANNING

6. Although no political decisions have been taken, US military planners have drafted options for the US Government to undertake an invasion of Iraq. In a "Running Start," military action could begin as early as November of this year, with no overt military build-up. Air strikes and support for opposition groups in Iraq would lead initially to small-scale land operations, with further

land forces deploying sequentially, ultimately overwhelming Iraqi forces and leading to the collapse of the Iraqi regime. A "Generated Start" would involve a longer build-up before any military action were taken, as early as January 2003. US military plans include no specifics on the strategic context either before or after the campaign. Currently the preference appears to be for the "Running Start." CDS will be ready to brief Ministers in more detail.

7. US plans assume, as a minimum, the use of British bases in Cyprus and Diego Garcia. This means that legal base issues would arise virtually whatever option Ministers choose with regard to UK participation.

THE VIABILITY OF THE PLANS

8. The Chiefs of Staff have discussed the viability of US military plans. Their initial view is that there are a number of questions which would have to be answered before they could assess whether the plans are sound. Notably these include the realism of the "Running Start," the extent to which the plans are proof against Iraqi counter-attack using chemical or biological weapons and the robustness of US assumptions about the bases and about Iraqi (un)willingness to fight.

UK MILITARY CONTRIBUTION

9. The UK's ability to contribute forces depends on the details of the US military planning and the time available to prepare and deploy them. The MOD is examining how the UK might contribute to US-led action. The options range from deployment of a Division (i.e., Gulf War–sized contribution plus naval and air forces) to making available bases. It is already clear that the UK could not generate a Division in time for an operation in January 2003, unless publicly visible decisions were taken very soon. Maritime and air forces could be deployed in time, provided adequate basing arrangements could be made. The lead times involved in preparing for UK military involvement include the procurement of Urgent Operational Requirements, for which there is no financial provision.

THE CONDITIONS NECESSARY FOR MILITARY ACTION

10. Aside from the existence of a viable military plan we consider the following conditions necessary for military action and UK participation: justification/legal base; an international coalition; a quiescent Israel/Palestine; a positive risk/benefit assessment; and the preparation of domestic opinion.

JUSTIFICATION

11. US views of international law vary from that of the UK and the international community. Regime change per se is not a proper basis for military action under international law. But regime change could result from action that is otherwise lawful. We would regard the use of force against Iraq, or any other state, as lawful if exercised in the right of individual or collective self-defence, if carried out to avert an overwhelming humanitarian catastrophe, or authorised by the UN Security Council. A detailed consideration of the legal issues, prepared earlier this year, is at Annex A. The legal position would depend on the precise circumstances at the time. Legal bases for an invasion of Iraq are in principle conceivable in both the first two instances but would be difficult to establish because of, for example, the tests of immediacy and proportionality. Further legal advice would be needed on this point.

12. This leaves the route under the UNSC resolutions on weapons inspectors. Kofi Annan has held three rounds of meetings with Iraq in an attempt to persuade them to admit the UN weapons inspectors. These have made no substantive progress; the Iraqis are deliberately obfuscating. Annan has downgraded

the dialogue but more pointless talks are possible. We need to persuade the UN and the international community that this situation cannot be allowed to continue ad infinitum. We need to set a deadline, leading to an ultimatum. It would be preferable to obtain backing of a UNSCR for any ultimatum and early work would be necessary to explore with Kofi Annan and the Russians, in particular, the scope for achieving this.

13. In practice, facing pressure of military action, Saddam is likely to admit weapons inspectors as a means of forestalling it. But once admitted, he would not allow them to operate freely. UNMOVIC (the successor to UNSCOM) will take at least six months after entering Iraq to establish the monitoring and verification system under Resolution 1284 necessary to assess whether Iraq is meeting its obligations. Hence, even if UN inspectors gained access today, by January 2003 they would at best only just be completing setting up. It is possible that they will encounter Iraqi obstruction during this period, but this more likely when they are fully operational.

14. It is just possible that an ultimatum could be cast in terms which Saddam would reject (because he is unwilling to accept unfettered access) and which would not be regarded as unreasonable by the international community. However, failing that

(or an Iraqi attack) we would be most unlikely to achieve a legal base for military action by January 2003.

AN INTERNATIONAL COALITION

15. An international coalition is necessary to provide a military platform and desirable for political purposes.

16. US military planning assumes that the US would be allowed to use bases in Kuwait (air and ground forces), Jordan, in the Gulf (air and naval forces) and UK territory (Diego Garcia and our bases in Cyprus). The plans assume that Saudi Arabia would withhold co-operation except granting military over-flights. On the assumption that military action would involve operations in the Kurdish area in the North of Iraq, the use of bases in Turkey would also be necessary.

17. In the absence of UN authorisation, there will be problems in securing the support of NATO and EU partners. Australia would be likely to participate on the same basis as the UK. France might be prepared to take part if she saw military action as inevitable. Russia and China, seeking to improve their US relations, might set aside their misgivings if sufficient attention

were paid to their legal and economic concerns. Probably the best we could expect from the region would be neutrality. The US is likely to restrain Israel from taking part in military action. In practice, much of the international community would find it difficult to stand in the way of the determined course of the US hegemon. However, the greater the international support, the greater the prospects of success.

A QUIESCENT ISRAEL-PALESTINE

18. The Israeli re-occupation of the West Bank has dampened Palestinian violence for the time being but is unsustainable in the long term and stoking more trouble for the future. The Bush speech was at best a half step forward. We are using the Palestinian reform agenda to make progress, including a resumption of political negotiations. The Americans are talking of a ministerial conference in November or later. Real progress towards a viable Palestinian state is the best way to undercut Palestinian extremists and reduce Arab antipathy to military action against Saddam Hussein. However, another upsurge of Palestinian/Israeli violence is highly likely. The co-incidence of such an upsurge with the preparations for military action against Iraq cannot be ruled out. Indeed Saddam would use

continuing violence in the Occupied Territories to bolster popular Arab support for his regime.

BENEFITS/RISKS

19. Even with a legal base and a viable military plan, we would still need to ensure that the benefits of action outweigh the risks. In particular, we need to be sure that the outcome of the military action would match our objective as set out in paragraph 5 above. A post-war occupation of Iraq could lead to a protracted and costly nation-building exercise. As already made clear, the US military plans are virtually silent on this point. Washington could look to us to share a disproportionate share of the burden. Further work is required to define more precisely the means by which the desired endstate would be created, in particular what form of government might replace Saddam Hussein's regime and the timescale within which it would be possible to identify a successor. We must also consider in greater detail the impact of military action on other UK interests in the region.

DOMESTIC OPINION

20. Time will be required to prepare public opinion in the UK that it is necessary to take military action against Saddam Hussein. There would also need to be a substantial effort to secure the support of Parliament. An information campaign will be needed which has to be closely related to an overseas information campaign designed to influence Saddam Hussein, the Islamic World and the wider international community. This will need to give full coverage to the threat posed by Saddam Hussein, including his WMD, and the legal justification for action.

TIMESCALES

21. Although the US military could act against Iraq as soon as November, we judge that a military campaign is unlikely to start until January 2003, if only because of the time it will take to reach consensus in Washington. That said, we judge that for climactic reasons, military action would need to start by January 2003, unless action were deferred until the following autumn.

22. As this paper makes clear, even this timescale would present problems. This means that:

(a) We need to influence US consideration of the military plans before President Bush is briefed on 4 August, through contacts between the Prime Minister and the President and at other levels;

[*The leaked version of the document ends here.*]

Mark Danner has been reporting on and writing about foreign affairs for twenty years. A longtime staff writer at *The New Yorker* and a regular contributor to *The New York Review of Books*, Danner has covered Central America, Haiti, the Balkans, and Iraq, among other stories. He is the author of *Torture and Truth: America, Abu Ghraib, and the War on Terror*, *The Road to Illegitimacy: One Reporter's Travels Through the 2000 Florida Vote Recount*, and *The Massacre at El Mozote: A Parable of the Cold War*. His writing has been recognized with many honors, including three Overseas Press Awards, a National Magazine Award, and an Emmy. In 1999, Danner was named a MacArthur Fellow. He is Professor of Journalism at the University of California at Berkeley and Henry R. Luce Professor of Human Rights and Journalism at Bard College. Danner divides his time between New York and San Francisco.

Frank Rich is an Associate Editor and columnist at *The New York Times*.